Underdog Entrepreneurs

"Professor Morgan provides a powerful contribution on an extremely timely topic. Innovative entrepreneurs are a scarce resource, and increasing the success of diverse entrepreneurs will boost the whole society. This book will certainly benefit minority entrepreneurs, but should also be on the reading list of practitioners, policy makers, and all scholars interested in minority and immigrant entrepreneurship."
—Sari Pekkala Kerr, *Senior Research Scientist at Wellesley College, USA; Research Economist, National Bureau of Economic Research (NBER)*

"Horatio Morgan has succeeded in presenting a compelling and accessible guide to the challenges that entrepreneurs from marginalized groups face, and evidence-based strategies for overcoming these challenges. His writing draws on theory, research, and case studies to provide valuable step-by-step advice about the skills and strategies "underdog" entrepreneurs can use to achieve their goals. *Underdog Entrepreneurs* fills an important gap and will be quoted for years to come by successful entrepreneurs from marginalized groups who have benefited from Morgan's engrossing book."
—Victoria M. Esses, *Professor of Psychology, Director of the Centre for Research on Migration and Ethnic Relations, Co-Chair and Principal Investigator of the Pathways to Prosperity Partnership, University of Western Ontario, CA; Co-editor of Twenty-First-Century Immigration to North America: Newcomers in Turbulent Times*

Horatio M. Morgan

Underdog Entrepreneurs

A Framework of Success for Marginalized and Minority Innovators

Horatio M. Morgan
Ryerson University
Toronto, ON, Canada

ISBN 978-3-030-20407-5   ISBN 978-3-030-20408-2 (eBook)
https://doi.org/10.1007/978-3-030-20408-2

© The Editor(s) (if applicable) and The Author(s), under exclusive licence to Springer Nature Switzerland AG 2020
This work is subject to copyright. All rights are solely and exclusively licensed by the Publisher, whether the whole or part of the material is concerned, specifically the rights of translation, reprinting, reuse of illustrations, recitation, broadcasting, reproduction on microfilms or in any other physical way, and transmission or information storage and retrieval, electronic adaptation, computer software, or by similar or dissimilar methodology now known or hereafter developed.
The use of general descriptive names, registered names, trademarks, service marks, etc. in this publication does not imply, even in the absence of a specific statement, that such names are exempt from the relevant protective laws and regulations and therefore free for general use.
The publisher, the authors and the editors are safe to assume that the advice and information in this book are believed to be true and accurate at the date of publication. Neither the publisher nor the authors or the editors give a warranty, express or implied, with respect to the material contained herein or for any errors or omissions that may have been made. The publisher remains neutral with regard to jurisdictional claims in published maps and institutional affiliations.

Cover illustration: © Claudia Velazquez / EyeEm / Getty

This Palgrave Macmillan imprint is published by the registered company Springer Nature Switzerland AG
The registered company address is: Gewerbestrasse 11, 6330 Cham, Switzerland

In loving memory of my father Clifton Roy Morgan, an underdog who always dared to smile and think big.

Preface

Sitting at the edge of his bed, an elbow resting on his raised knee, a frail-looking Mr. Wang Enlin leans forward.[1] Now in his sixties, he has short, flattened hair with streaks of gray, and his clean-shaven face makes his cheekbones appear more pronounced. Beneath his bushy eyebrows, his sunken eyes could hold you in a steely stare.

In his small room, a wrench rests on his bed close to two upright rusty gas cylinders; a picture of a youthful man in military uniform hangs on a wall; and a stack of law books tilts to the left on the floor. This is an odd collection for a man who dropped out of school at age ten and took up farming in the village of Yushutun.

This village is on the outskirts of Qiqihar, one of the larger cities in the Heilongjiang province, Northeast China. Although its residents sometimes have to deal with extreme cold and heat in the winter and summer, this is not what's on their minds these days. It's Qiqihar Chemical Group (QCG).

This company is a subsidiary of China's largest state-owned chemical company. Under questionable circumstances, it was allowed to use almost 29 hectares of land as a waste site for collecting a cocktail of toxic substances from its Polyvinyl chloride (PVC) production. Poorly managed and virtually unchecked, the copious amount of waste at this site has now crystalized into white stony-looking dross. Less visible are the dangerous substances that are penetrating the grounds, and seeping toward water sources.

The air in the village is no longer crisp and fresh. The water from a nearby well is now contaminated. When villagers look at the landscape from their windows, they no longer see a delightful array of grass and shrubs in varying shades of green. And when they toil in a corn field, it no longer promises a bountiful harvest.

Already suffering from lung problems, Wang couldn't just cough and look the other way. Instead, he organized a senior citizen group to take up environmental issues in the village. Once a place for light conversations and laughter over a card game, his house had now become a command post for privately working out their case against QCG. The damning evidence is still in the air; and the waste site is still there for all to smell, taste and see. But when Wang asked lawyers and government officials for help, they turned him away.

Around 2001, he decided to study law on his own and take on QCG in court. This was no easy feat because he was already a middle-aged man without formal education. But the stack of law books in his house tells us that he sought legal knowledge like a drowning man gasping for air.

From the day he started out, and certainly now, Wang knew that it would be difficult to get compensation from QCG, let alone stop it from operating in the village. But after a six-year struggle without formal legal assistance, he and his fellow villagers were lucky to gain support from the Center for Legal Assistance to Pollution Victims in 2007.

Multiple inspections of the waste site followed; and piles of paperwork grew into mountains. Seven years later, there was something to cheer about, albeit in a tempered way: The Ministry of Environmental Protection formally acknowledged the case against QCG. Even in 2015 when a local court officially accepted the case, it was still too soon to celebrate.

The justice system gave Wang a more compelling reason to rejoice in 2017. It ruled that QCG should clean up the waste site, and compensate Wang and other villagers for the farm-related losses they had suffered.

But in a flash, QCG wielded its sword of appeal. The justice system responded by rolling back the legal victory that the villagers had tasted.

Wang now contemplates his decision to file an appeal in the presence of a reporter and friends.

"We will absolutely win. The law is on our side," said Wang.[2]

Perhaps you can relate to the plight of Wang. He's an underdog; yet, he's not acting like one.

In this book, I shine the spotlight on innovative underdog entrepreneurs in a science- and technology-driven Western world. Unlike their traditionally dominant white male peers in Silicon Valley and elsewhere, they come from actual or self-perceived marginalized and minority groups—including immigrants, refugees, women, blacks, Hispanics, and Asians. Unfortunately, too many of them are pushed into entrepreneurship; and oftentimes, with little knowledge, if any, of the code-breaking skills they need to succeed against the odds.

But this book has now tipped the balance in their favor by uncovering these skills and so much more. It does so by proposing a framework that helps them analyze common obstacles, and develop personal qualities and strategies to overcome them. Although other authors offer practical advice to minority entrepreneurs, they are yet to integrate insights gleaned from diverse success stories into a coherent framework. By providing such a framework, this book enables marginalized and minority entrepreneurs to precisely understand why and how a growth mindset, valuable knowledge from formal education, strategic identity orientation, and social and political skills can help them succeed in the face of what may be called the *outsider problem*—as reflected in limited access, if any, to powerful mainstream networks, lack of relevant know-how, stereotype-driven discrimination and stereotype threat.

This proposed framework comes from insights and evidence distilled from multiple fields, combined with a fresh look at the familiar stories of initially marginalized business leaders,[3] such as Indra Nooyi (former CEO of PepsiCo, United States), Jack Ma (Co-Founder, Alibaba Group, China), Hilary Devey (CEO and Chairman, Pall-Ex Group, United Kingdom), and Mike Lazaridis (Co-Founder and former Co-CEO, BlackBerry, Canada). It also features the less known, but equally inspiring stories of others, including Tahani Aburaneh (Real Estate Investment Expert, Canada), Aquilino Flores (Founder, Topitop, Peru), Aisha Addo (Founder, Power to Girls Foundation, DriveHer, Canada), Tan Le (Founder and CEO, EMOTIV, Australia/United States), Bimpe Nkontchou (Managing Principal, W8 Advisory, United Kingdom), Hussein Shaker (Co-Founder, MigrantHire, Germany), and Clarence Wooten (Serial Entrepreneur; Founder and CEO, STEAM Role and other ventures, United States).

In a nutshell, this book helps marginalized and minority entrepreneurs achieve and sustain success. It not only pinpoints their underlying problem but also helps them solve it by doing several things better—like learning and developing capabilities, creating lasting positive first impressions, becoming less vulnerable to discrimination and negative stereotypes, cultivating and using networks, recognizing and managing their multiple self-identities, accumulating power, using government support, and developing higher-order mental skills. When they improve in these critical areas, they will become more adept at spotting attractive opportunities in a science- and technology-driven global marketplace, developing strategies to exploit these opportunities, and mobilizing the resources required to execute these strategies. Ultimately, they will transcend their underdog status and thrive.

Toronto, ON   Horatio M. Morgan

Notes

1. This account is not meant to serve as a biography. I have tried to recreate the events, places, settings, personal descriptions and conversations based on publicly available information, including: Tracy You for Mailonline, "Farmer spends 16 years studying law by himself so he could sue a powerful chemical firm for 'polluting his land'—and he wins the first round," *The Daily Mail* online (February 6, 2017); NDTV, "Man Dropped Out Of School, Taught Himself Law to Take on China's Largest Chemical Firm" (November 12, 2017); International POPs (Persistent Organic Pollutants) Elimination Network (IPEN) and Green Beagle, *China Chemical Safety Case Study: Qihua PVC plant in Qiqihar, Heilongjiang Province* (European Union, January 2015).
2. Primary source of quote: NDTV, "Man Dropped Out of School, Taught Himself Law to Take on China's Largest Chemical Firm" (November 12, 2017).
3. Previous entrepreneurship research has similarly proposed conceptual frameworks by building on theoretical insights and illustrative cases. For example, see the following work: Peter Vogel, "From Venture Idea to Venture Opportunity," *Entrepreneurship Theory and Practice*, vol. 41, no. 6 (2017), pp. 943–971.

Acknowledgments

As I reflect on the winding road that led me to this book, I recognize that far more people deserve credit than I can list here. But I hope my rippling feelings of gratitude will reach everyone who has helped me gather and transform scattered facts, ideas and experiences into a lively and insightful book worth reading.

When I think about the foundational work that went into it, Helen Guri readily comes to mind. Thanks to her superb editorial assistance and encouragement, I was able to take an earlier manuscript to the next level.

I'm also grateful to the many people at Palgrave Macmillan who were involved in the review, development, production and distribution of this book. I especially thank Marcus Ballenger, the Commissioning Editor, for his assistance and early vote of confidence in my proposed book. I acknowledge two anonymous reviewers for providing complimentary and constructive feedback; Hemalatha Arumugam for capably managing the production of the book; and Jacqueline Young for providing guidance during the entire publication process.

Turning to my colleagues and friends, I thank Nadine Förster (IQ Information Centre on Migrant Entrepreneurship, Germany) for inspiring me to write this book much sooner than I had planned. Since co-chairing a 2017 workshop on refugee entrepreneurship in The Hague, we have had refreshing conversations on some of the very ideas that I share in this book.

I thank Christopher A. D. Charles (University of the West Indies, Jamaica, West Indies), Asher Alkoby (Ryerson University, Canada), and

Murtaza Haider (Ryerson University, Canada) for helpful feedback on relevant issues.

I also acknowledge Nadine Habib (Ryerson University, Canada), whose generosity and remarkable journalism skills have made our talks about this book easy and meaningful.

I thank Jock Collins, Dina Petrakis, Tatjana Lukić-Co and Katherine Watson for sharing information on refugee entrepreneurs in Australia. They have also helped me understand the supportive role that Settlement Services International plays through its Ignite Small Business Start Ups program.

The growth and development of a scholar call for collegial, talented and committed research partners, among other things. I have been fortunate to have co-authors with these qualities. I thank Sui Sui (Ryerson University, Canada), Matthias Baum (Technische Universität Kaiserslautern, Germany), Shavin Malhotra (University of Waterloo, Canada) and Pengcheng ("Phil") Zhu (University of San Diego, United States) for the positive role they have played in my scholarly work and development. Some of the ideas that I have developed in this book are based on our co-authored research.

I have benefited from the generosity of others long before I wrote this book. Karen Campbell Gombele is one of them. She is one of the most talented English-literature teachers I know. My early fascination with words can be traced back to the liberation I sensed in her when she read and interpreted classic literature books and poetry. I would later learn that writing can be just as liberating. I thank Karen for enriching my life in these ways.

I'd like to close by thanking my family. I'm especially grateful to Sharlene Gayle Morgan and our two daughters, Kerene and Keleese, for listening to my half-baked stories and providing love and support along the way.

I thank my Sisters (Maxine, Vinnette, Sheryl, Panzel, Verona and Sereen) for being there for me in their own unique way. I also acknowledge my late sister, Marlene, who would have been thrilled to celebrate this book with me.

Special thanks to Dennis V. Brown and Grace Brown for the parental role they played in my life when it mattered most. I'm forever indebted to them.

Finally, I stand and praise my mom, Dorothy Velma Morgan, for her indomitable spirit, guidance and everlasting love.

Contents

1 Introduction: Underdog Entrepreneurs Are Everywhere   1

Part I   The Outsider Problem   19

2 Being on the Outside of Powerful Mainstream Networks   21

3 Lacking Relevant Know-How   35

4 Being Subject to Stereotype-Driven Discrimination and Stereotype Threat   43

Part II   Code-Breaking Skills   63

5 A Growth Mindset   65

6 Valuable Knowledge from Formal Education   73

7 Strategic Identity Orientation   83

8 Complementary Social and Political Skills   93

Part III	Putting It All Together and Drawing Lessons	105
9	An Integrative Framework	107
10	Commit to Ongoing Learning and Capability Development	111
11	Strategically Cultivate Mutually Beneficial Networks	117
12	Experiment with Self-Identities; Don't Be Rigidly Defined by Them	123
13	Strategically Accumulate Power and Appropriately Use It	131
14	Strategically Target and Use Government Support	139
15	Cultivate Higher-Order Mental Skills	145
16	Conclusion: Underdog Entrepreneurs' Most Enduring Asset	149
17	Epilogue: What Journey Brought Me Here?	151
Index		159

CHAPTER 1

Introduction: Underdog Entrepreneurs Are Everywhere

Another frantic day at PepsiCo's corporate headquarters had ended. With the parking lots almost vacant, its Purchase, New York grounds and gardens appeared to cover a much wider area than the estimated 150 acres of land. It was after 9 p.m., but light and movements could be seen from an office: Indra Nooyi's.[1]

She was seated in a black leather chair at a rectangular desk with a wood-like finish. As she reached for a yellow jacketed binder, bulging with papers, other binders vied for her attention. About an arm's length to her left, an Aquafina brand of bottled water also sat on her desk and patiently waited. Behind her, framed pictures of her two daughters, Preetha and Tara, and her husband, Raj, sat on another matching desk against a wall.

On this particular night, Indra was reviewing files on Quaker Oats, PepsiCo's recent acquisition at a whopping price of roughly $13 billion. Combining the operations of both companies was a challenge, and she wanted to get it right.

The ring of the phone gave her a well-deserved break.

When Indra answered, she immediately recognized the voice of Steven Reinemund, PepsiCo's CEO at the time.

"Indra, we're gonna announce you as the new CEO and put you on the board of directors of PepsiCo," said Steven.[2]

Although the year was 2006, news of Indra's promotion was a remarkable development in corporate America: she had become one of only 11 female CEOs who headed Fortune 500 companies—America's 500 largest private and public companies based on reported revenues.³ Her appointment as PepsiCo's CEO was particularly extraordinary because there was only one non-white Fortune 500 female CEO before her—Avon Products' Andrea Jung, a Chinese-American.

Like the rest of corporate America, Indra needed time to come to terms with her phenomenal accomplishment. Although she had good reasons to be optimistic about landing the top-manager job before Steven confirmed it, nothing was guaranteed. Several years earlier, he had made it clear that PepsiCo's entry into fast-growing urban and ethnic communities across the United States was a priority.⁴ He pursued this goal by promoting a diversified senior management team that these communities could identify with. Such a management team began to take shape as Steven intensified PepsiCo's commitment to hire, promote and retain more senior executives from marginalized groups.

Indra could have interpreted these developments to mean that she and her minority peers had a better chance of getting to the CEO level. At the same time, she might have felt that it was still difficult to get there. After all, she had previously suggested that she faced more barriers than her peers: "If you are a woman and especially a person of colour, there are two strikes against you … Immigrant, person of colour and woman—that is three strikes against you. So I have to work extra hard. More hours, yes. More sacrifices and trade-offs, yes. That has been my journey."⁵

But when Steven broke the news about her promotion that night, she had other things to think about.

I imagine she reflected on her humble beginnings in Chennai, India. Perhaps she remembered the many times she saw her mother, Shantha, praying for the family up to five hours a day; or the majestic Tirupati temple.

Since her father was away on business most of the time, Shantha had picked up the slack. And she did so zealously. Like others of South Indian, Tamil-speaking, Brahmin heritage, Shantha demanded academic excellence from her children; something Indra, her sister, Chandrika, and brother, Narayan, had all come to see as a normal way of life. It didn't bother Indra that she was expected to get 100 percent in Math. And she especially liked the challenge of debating Chandrika in imaginary presidential races at dinner time. A single vote by Shantha would decide the winner.

Perhaps she recalled that her mother had wanted her to get married by 18. But any stress induced by this memory would have been short-lived because her father and grandfather had protested. That was all the cover she needed to freely pursue her dreams.

These dreams would take her all the way to the United States in 1978. At 23 years old, Indra was ready to chart her course as a new immigrant with $500 in her pocket and a scholarship from Yale University. She worked part time and boldly took on graduate studies in management at Yale School of Management.

Two years later, she was ready to take on corporate America, a journey that eventually led her to PepsiCo in 1994.

She had already worked there for 12 years when Steven called that night. But after she hung up the phone, she knew her time had come to lead an iconic American company.

There were still untouched binders to keep her at the office past midnight. But she left shortly after the call, feeling much better than when she first arrived there.

* * *

Much of what we know about Indra tells us that she is a minority-female-immigrant senior executive who is worthy of admiration.

By her own admission, she had faced multiple barriers as a woman, a person of color and an immigrant. Throughout her career, she tried to cope by adhering to a strong work ethic, fueled by an "immigrant mentality."[6]

In other words, she was pressed to work harder and deliver better results than others because she always felt insecure about her job as an immigrant: "the job can be taken away at any time, so make sure you earn it every day ... when immigrants come here, they have no safety net—zero. I landed here with $500 in my pocket. I had no one here to pay for me," she once said.[7]

It is clear that marginalized and minority senior executives can identify with, and learn from, Indra. However, it is much less clear what she adds to a discourse on the common obstacles faced by marginalized and minority entrepreneurs, and how to solve them. To begin to see why, we need to first establish a common understanding of entrepreneurship.

It might come as a surprise to some people, but there is no general agreement on what counts as entrepreneurship, or who should be considered entrepreneurs. However, the late Austrian economist Joseph Schumpeter provided a good starting point when he portrayed entrepreneurs as innovators.[8] In this role, they are expected to do well at two basic things: recombining existing knowledge or ideas in ways that lead to novel ideas; and then converting such ideas in new or improved products, services, technologies or processes that create value for their companies.

When they perform these tasks very well, they may produce radical innovations that disrupt entire industries. This disruption is often manifested in the re-ordering of established ways of doing business, patterns of resource flows and consumer demand, and the mix of winners and losers.[9] For example, when Uber introduced its new digital, ride-sharing business model, it rapidly transformed the transport industry by virtually displacing traditional taxi operators, and enabling passengers to switch places with transport service providers when they want to do so.[10]

If we accept the view that innovation is the essence of entrepreneurship, then those who excel at it are entrepreneurs, independent of whether they create a new venture, or lead an established company. This means that CEOs at Fortune 500 companies who drive innovation can be viewed as entrepreneurs, or more precisely as intrapreneurs—since they enact innovative ideas that create value for large corporations rather than new ventures.

This brings us back to Indra. She would easily qualify as an intrapreneur during her tenure at PepsiCo. Faced with declining demand for soda with high sugar content, she could have fallen for a quiet life by merely trying to slow down the decline—possibly by ramping up the advertising budget for the existing portfolio of sugar-laden beverages.[11] This move might have been sufficient to deliver satisfactory results, appease skeptical investors and secure rock-solid support from PepsiCo's board of directors. But Indra went for a more demanding and riskier move by acting on her entrepreneurial orientation.

She had anticipated and sought to meet consumers' demand for healthier food and drink choices by promoting paradigm-shifting innovations in these areas.[12] At the time, impressive results weren't expected to materialize soon. This made her a target for disgruntled activist investors and other members of the top management team who had disagreed with her strategy.[13] She would also put the patience of PepsiCo's supportive board to the test.

The decision to boldly explore new possibilities, rather than go with proven products, could have ended badly for Indra. She had moved from middle management into top management faster than her peers.[14] But she was now at risk of joining a growing list of female CEOs who were forced to prematurely leave their companies.[15] Fortunately, the risk paid off for everyone. PepsiCo's growing portfolio of healthy offerings has substantially strengthened its competitive position in the food and beverage industry on a global scale.[16] When Indra stepped down as PepsiCo's CEO in 2018, she may have lasted longer at the top of a global company than most of her peers ever will.[17]

Going beyond her demonstrated entrepreneurial orientation, Indra deserves special attention because her appeal to the immigrant mentality as a motivating force isn't an isolated experience. On the contrary, it is at work in many foreign-born entrepreneurs in advanced Western countries.

Consider Tahani Aburaneh, a leading expert on real estate investing and entrepreneur in Canada.[18] When her Palestinian parents sent her off to Canada in 1981, she was a 15-year-old teenager on her way to an arranged marriage with her male cousin. She didn't speak English, and the life she knew had unfolded in a refugee camp in Amman, Jordan. Determined to learn English and improve herself, she enrolled in a language course and went on to a business administration and management program at Conestoga College in Kitchener, Ontario. At age 21, she was writing college exams while on the verge of delivering her first child.

When she finished college, she couldn't find acceptable work. But pressed to support herself and her family, she kept trying by taking on contract work assignments. Eventually she met Lou Pereira, a real estate brokerage owner. He sold her on the idea that she had exceptional social skills that could serve well as a real estate investment agent. With hard work and determination, the course of her life and prospects fared much better than she might have imagined.

For another example, consider Hussein Shaker, a Syrian refugee from Aleppo in Berlin, Germany.[19] When he arrived there in March 2015, he had joined more than one million asylum seekers. Hussein had survived a dangerous journey, and uncomfortable nights sleeping on a basketball court. But getting his asylum application approved and learning to speak German were still daunting challenges ahead. Given his computer programming skills, he should have appealed to German tech companies because they have as many as 200,000 unfilled vacancies each year. But like other non-German-speaking refugees, his chance of getting an offer from these companies was low.

While taking German-language training, Hussein reluctantly accepted a part-time position at a call center that made use of his competence in Arabic. But another door opened when a friend introduced him to a Norwegian entrepreneur, Remi Mekki, in Berlin. He learned for the first time that some tech companies were willing to hire English-speaking refugees with computer programming skills. This was good news because many refugees were more comfortable with English than German. By the end of 2015, Hussein helped create the first permanent and meaningful job for himself and others by co-founding the recruitment platform, MigrantHire, with Remi and two other partners.

For an example from Australia, consider Tan Le, the founder and CEO of the San Francisco-based, brain-monitoring technology company, EMOTIV.[20] Before celebrating her first birthday, Tan was already on track for a difficult life in Vietnam under a repressive communist regime. Fearing persecution, many Vietnamese with anti-communist sentiments, or minority religion status, secretly hatched escape plans. In 1976, a small fishing boat crossed the choppy waves of the Arafura Sea. From its hold, five Vietnamese asylum seekers quietly crept out on to the shores of the Darwin harbor in Australia. The arrival of the "boat people" had begun.

In 1981, a four-year-old Tan, and her younger sister, mother and grandmother would become boat people as well. After a five-day journey by boat, they ended up at a refugee camp in Malaysia. They would resettle in Footscray Melbourne three months later. With fears of pirates and captivity now behind her, Tan would embark on a new journey with an enterprising mother who sacrificed much for her well-being and education.

At age 16, Tan was on track to advance her education at Monash University. Five years later, she had a bachelor's degree in law and commerce. Leading up to this point, she significantly contributed to the Melbourne Vietnamese community, for which she won the 1998 Young Australian of the Year. In 2003, she made her mark as an entrepreneur when she co-founded Emotiv Systems, a neuro-engineering company that facilitates the observation of digital media inputs from the brain. Seven years later, Tan's entrepreneurial journey would take her outside Australia to San Francisco, where she continues to lead Emotiv.

You can find moving stories of immigrant, migrant or refugee entrepreneurs in so many places around the world. They have long sought to settle and rebuild their lives in rich and safe countries such as the United States, Canada, Australia and the United Kingdom. In recent years, many people have been forced to leave their counties unprepared, and oftentimes with little hope of returning soon.

In 2015, there were at least 65 million of such migrants, roughly half of whom came from the Middle East and Africa.[21] As asylum seekers, many migrants have taken on a perilous journey in search of a better country. While non-European countries (i.e., Turkey, Pakistan, Lebanon, Iran) received most of the last wave of asylum seekers, the number of asylum applications reached unprecedented levels in European Union (EU) countries such as Germany, Sweden, Austria, France, Italy, and the United Kingdom.[22]

As foreign-born individuals in the West, immigrants, migrants and refugees all have to deal with the unfavorable judgments that others make about their language skills, foreign credentials, cultural practices, ability to integrate, and so on.[23] And of course, they may be seriously disadvantaged based on these judgments alone. Thus, even when equally capable immigrants and native-born professionals pursue the same vacant positions or entrepreneurial opportunities, their native-born peers are more likely to come away as winners.

Hard evidence generally supports the view that immigrants struggle a lot, and for too long in their Western host country. Consider the Canadian context. The big picture is that they earn about three-fifth of what their Canadian-born peers earn as workers.[24] So there's an income gap. In theory, this gap could disappear in a few years if immigrants make steady progress—that is, quickly land a well-paying job that makes use of their experience and skills, or start a thriving business. But this is not what we see when we look at the data for Canada and other developed countries, such as the United States, Australia, and Germany.

Over time, the income gap tends to narrow when immigrants have highly marketable skills, or a sound understanding of the way of life in these countries.[25] But many will earn less than their native-born peers over their entire lifetime.[26] For all these reasons, immigrants and other foreign-born individuals are predisposed to an underdog status in the West. Many of them will turn to entrepreneurship. However, it is unclear whether doing so will improve their economic and social conditions.

But foreign-born individuals are not the only ones who might feel like underdogs. Anyone can feel this way if their personal attributes seem to work against them when they are seeking a job or promotion; or trying to build a business. There are underdog stories to be told based on race too.

Consider Clarence Wooten, an African-American serial entrepreneur.[27] As a kid growing up between Baltimore's inner city and suburbs, he often passed his time playing on video game consoles such as Atari, ColecoVision and Commodore. But his interest in video games wasn't what set him apart from his peers in high school. The business cards he carried certainly did. In addition, he was involved in family-run businesses, including assisted-living residence and residential rental property operations.

Outside his family circle, his role models include Bill Gates and the late corporate lawyer Reginald F. Lewis from Baltimore—who used to shrug off the emphasis others placed on his African-American background as his TLC ("The Lewis Corporation") empire propelled him into the billionaire club in the 1980s.

With these influences at work in his life, a young, computer savvy Clarence was eager to take a chance on his ideas; and ultimately, himself. He was directly involved in the creation of several business start-ups, such as Envision Designs and Metamorphosis Studios, before he received his associate degree in architecture at the Community College of Baltimore County in 1993. By the time he received a business and management degree at John Hopkins University in 1998, he was already on track for a breakthrough business venture: he had co-founded and led ImageCafe.com. This internet company enabled small business owners with newly registered domain names to quickly, and cheaply develop their websites by downloading pre-built customizable templates. Only seven months later, he and his business partners sold the company to Network Solutions/Verisign for $23 million. By 2006, he would move on to another venture, Groupsite.com, a social media platform that helps private groups or communities to collaborate online.

In another bold move, Clarence relocated to Palo Alto, Silicon Valley in 2011. Since then, he has founded a number of ventures, including: Progressly, an enterprise platform for executing business processes and monitoring progress; VentureFund.io, a data-driven funding marketplace; and STEAM Role, a networking app that connects emerging and established S.T.E.A.M (Science, Technology, Engineering, Arts and Mathematics) professionals.

Despite his entrepreneurial orientation, Clarence has struggled to mobilize the resources he needs to turn his fledging ventures into mature tech companies. Research suggests that he belongs to a much larger group of black and Hispanic entrepreneurs that fare worse than their white peers in the world of business.[28]

In many cases, race and socioeconomic status combine to compound the obstacles faced by enterprising women and men alike. In particular, people can find it extremely difficult to mobilize resources to develop and grow a business when they come from low-income families, or have a low social status. The Peruvian economist Hernando de Soto provides insights on the poor in developing countries that offer clues about the harsh realities that their counterparts might face in the less developed regions of advanced Western countries. He reveals their plight by emphasizing that they have relatively little, if any, enforceable rights to the lands on which they toil, the homes in which they live, or the businesses they operate.[29] This can make it very difficult for them to mobilize basic resources to grow a business.

At age 13, Aquilino Flores was trying to make a living by washing cars and selling cotton T-shirts in various poverty-stricken places, or barrios, in Peru.[30] Those who knew Aquilino well might have written him off as another young peddler without promise. After all, he and his four brothers and sister were raised in the region of Huancavelica, southeast of Lima, Peru's capital city. Mercury-mining operations had once been the main source of employment for its residents. But by the 1960s, they were reduced to subsistence living on small farms with few livestock; and a handful of crops, such as potatoes and barley. Therefore, Aquilino had little to lose when he left for the barrios in greater Lima.

In the heart of Lima's Central Market, he would become a master at spotting the unmet clothing needs of working people and the emerging middle class. By 1983, ongoing efforts to identify and satisfy those needs at low prices and convenient locations culminated in the creation of Topitop, a family-owned clothing manufacturing business. With annual sales in excess of $100 million and more than 5000 employees, Topitop has become a leader in Peru's textile industry. In addition, it has secured substantial contract work with leading Western clothing brands.

There are many more stories to be told than we can take up in this book. Although I examine the entrepreneurial journeys of some marginalized and minority groups (i.e., immigrants, refugees, blacks, Asians, Hispanics or women) more comprehensively than others, the overarching point is that underdog entrepreneurs are everywhere.

They can emerge from different situations, places and times. In addition to the factors we have already considered, some entrepreneurs are disadvantaged because of their national identity, disabilities, sexual orientation, age, religion, or political affiliation. In some cases, their situations are so destitute that their underdog status is undeniable. In other cases, we have self-described underdog entrepreneurs who perceive their disadvantages to be many, and their opportunities to be few. Sometimes a single change—like moving to a new country, losing a job, or experiencing a business failure—in an otherwise comfortable life is all it takes to land someone into underdog territory.

It's one thing to bring together entrepreneurs from diverse marginalized and minority groups, it's another thing to analyze them and draw meaningful lessons. Standing in the way are individual- and group-related differences that can complicate an analysis of the common challenges they face, and common qualities and strategies that lead to success. We can see this analytical challenge more clearly when we think about entrepreneurship in a more comprehensive way.

Although entrepreneurship can unfold in new and existing companies led by innovators, business researchers predominantly focus on entrepreneurs who engage in innovative and risk-taking behaviors in the context of new ventures.[31] This means that the emphasis is on enterprising individuals who recognize opportunities, and create new ventures to exploit them.[32] Therefore, we have a situation where it is the act of registering and operating a new business that primarily counts. Yet, this business might offer few novel products or services, if any, that add value in the marketplace.

This situation can arise when individuals become what may be called "necessity entrepreneurs." Specifically, they start a business primarily because they cannot find acceptable work, or face major barriers in the job market.[33] To see what such barriers might look like, consider this hypothetical scenario.

DeShawn Myrie, Qian Leung and Jake Anderson are black, Asian and white, respectively; and all born and raised in the United States. They recently graduated from the University of Michigan with a bachelor's degree in accounting, and the same grade point average (GPA) of 3.9. In their final year, they had a six-month internship with a small accounting firm. They also happen to live in the same Beverly Hills neighborhood, an upscale suburb in Detroit. Now desperate to find a job in accounting, they've sent out more than 50 resumes to accounting firms in the United States and Canada.

Who do think is more likely to receive a call for an interview?

If you guessed Jake, you're on to something.

Here's why.

Compared with native-born white applicants, research tells us that American and Canadian companies call back proportionally fewer immigrant, black and Asian job applicants for interviews; and when they do, they seriously consider them for a limited range of positions (i.e., back office jobs, middle management or technical roles).[34]

When individuals from marginalized and minority groups struggle to find acceptable work, or advance their careers in the mainstream corporate world, they may very well become necessity entrepreneurs. Consider Bimpe Nkontchou, the Managing Principal of the London-based asset management and wealth advisory practice, W8 Advisory.[35]

When Bimpe left Nigeria for the United Kingdom (UK) in 1995, she had good reason to be optimistic about her future prospects in her newly adopted home country. After all, the life she had known was an extraordinary one. With both parents as medical doctors, Bimpe had an early exposure to a life of comfort and prestige.

She could have dreamt wildly about her career, but she fell for law. Her training to become a lawyer started at the University of Ife, where she earned a Bachelor of Laws degree. She later attended the University College London, where she obtained a Master's degree in Corporate and Commercial Law. Bimpe went on to become a seasoned corporate lawyer with substantial experience at prestigious law firms in Nigeria.

When she later arrived in the UK, she hadn't yet entertained the idea of venturing out on her own; instead, she wanted to work for a law firm that was at least on par with the ones she had worked in Nigeria. But things did not play out this way: "I soon realized that the opportunities in the legal services sector in the UK for an ethnic minority female were severely restricted and that my career would stagnate even if I was able to find a job in a prestigious English law firm in those conditions," she once said.[36]

Less than four years after arriving in the UK, Bimpe joined other necessity entrepreneurs by founding ADDIE & CO Solicitors in London.[37] This advisory practice primarily targets foreign investors and African companies that want to conduct business in certain parts of Africa (i.e., sub-Saharan Africa) and Europe.

Although Bimpe went on to become a successful entrepreneur, the story often ends differently for many necessity entrepreneurs. Specifically, they typically struggle because they're less prepared than others to formulate effective competitive strategies; and even less able to meet the resource requirements of such strategies.

The situation is markedly different for "opportunity entrepreneurs." Unlike necessity entrepreneurs, they often already have attractive job options, but choose to start a business because they spot a commercial opportunity that they can exploit under relatively ideal conditions.[38] Opportunity entrepreneurs are expected to fare relatively well because they have an enhanced ability to formulate and execute an effective competitive strategy.

These observations suggest that one has to be meticulous when analyzing entrepreneurs from diverse marginalized and minority groups (i.e., immigrants, refugees, women, blacks, Hispanics and Asians). I'm particularly mindful that they can differ in important ways, including their motivation for starting a business, available opportunities, innovation potential, personal wealth, capabilities, ability to mobilize resources, barriers, and so on.

For example, immigrants admitted into the United States or Canada based on their qualifications or business acumen are different from refugees admitted on humanitarian terms. The latter are likely to arrive with less verifiable credentials; and hence, will particularly struggle to find work and gain social acceptance in mainstream society. As a result, refugees are likely to be overrepresented among necessity entrepreneurs, compared with their more established immigrant counterparts.[39]

These issues reinforce the need for a careful analysis of diverse marginalized and minority entrepreneurs. At the same time, they make it even more worthwhile to figure out the common obstacles they face, and whether common approaches can address these obstacles.

NOTES

1. This account is not meant to serve as a biography. I have tried to recreate the events, places, settings, personal characteristics and conversations based on publicly available records, including: Gary Burnison, *No Fear of Failure: Real Stories of How Leaders Deal with Risk and Change* (San Francisco: Jossey-Bass, 2011, pp. 29–41); Richard Feloni, "Pepsi CEO Indra Nooyi explains how an unusual daily ritual her mom made her practice as a child changed her life," *Business Insider* (September 9, 2015); Lila MacLellan, "Religious CEOs: PepsiCo's Indra Nooyi," *Minyanville* (May 19, 2010); Andrew Ross Sorkin and Greg Winter, "PepsiCo Said to Acquire Quaker Oats for $13.4 Billion in Stock," *New York Times* (December 4, 2000); "Personal Side of Indra Nooyi," *The Economic Times* (interview with Nandan Nilekani) (February 7, 2007).
2. This reported conversation directly draws on the following account: "Why PepsiCo CEO Indra K. Nooyi Can't Have It All," *The Atlantic* (interview with David Bradley, Aspen Ideas Festival Monday, Aspen Institute, Colorado) (July 1, 2014).
3. At the time, the ten active female CEOs who preceded Indra are as follows: (1) Patricia A. Woertz, Archer Daniels Midland; (2) Margaret "Meg" Whitman, eBay; (3) Paula G. Rosput Reynolds, Safeco; (4) Brenda C. Barnes, Sara Lee; (5) Susan M. Cameron (Ivey), Reynolds American; (6) Mary F. Sammons, Rite Aid; (7) Patricia F. Russo, Lucent; (8) Anne M. Mulcahy, Xerox; (9) Andrea Fung, Avon Products; and (10) Marion O. Sandler, Golden West Financial. See the following sources: "Female CEOs of Fortune 500 Companies," KDM Engineering (Accessed August 10, 2018); Beth Kowitt, "PepsiCo's Indra Nooyi Is 'Concerned' Her Departure Will Leave So Few Female CEOs," *Fortune* (August 6, 2018).
4. David A. Thomas and Stephanie J. Creary, *Meeting the Diversity Challenge at PepsiCo: The Steve Reinemund Era*. Case: 9-410-024 (Boston, MA: Harvard Business School Publishing, 2009).
5. Anuj Chopra, "India's Glass Ceiling Hard to Crack," *The National* (June 12, 2011); Danny Samson, Timothy Donnet and Richard L. Daft, *Management*, 6th Asia-Pacific Edition (Sydney: Cengage Learning Australia Pty Limited, 2018, p. 548).

6. Gary Burnison (2011, p. 29).
7. Ibid.
8. Joseph A. Schumpeter, *Capitalism, Socialism, and Democracy* (New York: Harper & Bros, 1942).
9. Clayton M. Christensen, Rory McDonald, Elizabeth J. Altman and Jonathan E. Palmer, "Disruptive Innovation: An Intellectual History and Directions for Future Research," *Journal of Management Studies*, vol. 55, no. 7 (2018), pp. 1043–1078; Arun Kumaraswamy, Raghu Garud and Shahzad (Shaz) Ansari, "Perspectives on Disruptive Innovations," *Journal of Management Studies*, vol. 55, no. 7 (2018), pp. 1025–1042.
10. Ibid.
11. See the following sources for a deeper look into the tendency toward a quiet life, complacency or self-serving behavior among CEOs and other senior managers: Marianne Bertrand and Sendhil Mullainathan, "Enjoying the Quiet Life? Corporate Governance and Managerial Preferences," *Journal of Political Economy*, vol. 111, no. 5 (2003), pp. 1043–1075; Xavier Giroud and Holger M. Mueller, "Does Corporate Governance Matter in Competitive Industries?" *Journal of Financial Economics*, vol. 95, no. 3 (2010), pp. 312–331.
12. John Seabrook, "Snacks for a Fat Planet: PepsiCo Takes Stock of the Obesity Epidemic," *The New Yorker* (May 16, 2011); Kate Taylor, "How Pepsi's CEO Predicted the Death of Soda and Saved the Beverage Giant in the Process," *Business Insider* (August 6, 2018).
13. Geoff Colvin, "Indra Nooyi's Pepsi Challenge," *Fortune* (May 29, 2012); Mike Esterl, "PepsiCo Board Stands by Nooyi: After a Strategic Review, Marketing Dollars will Shift Back to Soda," *The Wall Street Journal* (January 13, 2013).
14. Ghazala Azmat and Rosa Ferrer, "Gender Gaps in Performance: Evidence from Young Lawyers," *Journal of Political Economy*, vol. 125, no. 5 (2017), pp. 1306–1355; Francine D. Blau and Lawrence M. Kahn, "Gender Differences in Pay," *Journal of Economic Perspectives*, vol. 14, no. 4 (2000), pp. 75–99; Alison Cook and Christy Glass, "Above the glass ceiling: When are women and racial/ethnic minorities promoted to CEO?" *Strategic Management Journal*, vol. 35, no. 7 (2014), pp. 1080–1089; David A. Cotter, Joan M. Hermsen, Seth Ovadia, Reeve Vanneman, "The Glass Ceiling Effect," *Social Forces*, vol. 80, no. 2 (2001), pp. 655–682; Marina Glogovac, "The Challenge for Women to Smash the Glass Ceiling," *The Globe and Mail* (March 24, 2017); Elizabeth H. Gorman and Julie A. Kmec, "Hierarchical Rank and Women's Organizational Mobility: Glass Ceilings in Corporate Law Firms," *American Journal of Sociology*, vol. 114, no. 5 (2009), pp. 1428–1474; Sue V. Rosser, *The Science Glass Ceiling: Academic Women Scientists and the Struggle to Succeed* (New York: Routledge, 2004).
15. Victoria L. Brescoll, Erica Dawson and Eric Luis Uhlmann, "Hard Won and Easily Lost: The Fragile Status of Leaders in Gender-Stereotype-

Incongruent Occupations," *Psychological Science*, vol. 21, no. 11 (2010), pp. 1640–1642; Vishal K. Gupta, Seonghee Han, Sandra C. Mortal, Sabatino (Dino) Silveri and Daniel B. Turban, "Do Women CEOs Face Greater Threat of Shareholder Activism Compared to Male CEOs? A Role Congruity Perspective," *Journal of Applied Psychology*, vol. 103, no. 2 (2018), pp. 228–236; Jennifer Reingold, "Why Top Women Are Disappearing from Corporate America," *Fortune* (September 16, 2018); Michelle K. Ryan and S. Alexander Haslam, "The Glass Cliff: Exploring the Dynamics Surrounding the Appointment of Women to Precarious Leadership Positions," *Academy of Management Review*, vol. 32, no. 2 (2007), pp. 549–572.
16. John Kell, "PepsiCo's Promise to Get Healthier Is Paying Off," *Fortune* (February 15, 2017).
17. Beth Kowitt, "PepsiCo's Indra Nooyi Is 'Concerned' Her Departure Will Leave So Few Female CEOs," *Fortune* (August 6, 2018); Rachel Siegel and Jena McGregor, "Indra Nooyi, One of the Few Minority Female CEOs in the U.S., Is Stepping Down as Head of Pepsi," *The Washington Post* (August 6, 2018).
18. Gail Johnson, "From Refugee to Real Estate Mogul: How Tahani Aburaneh Became a Self-Made Millionaire," *Yahoo Finance Canada* (March 8, 2018); "From refugee camp to status as millionaire," *Cambridge Times* (September 10, 2012).
19. Morgan Meaker, "The Syrian Who's Aiming to Get Refugees Jobs in Berlin's Booming Tech Scene," *The Guardian* (May 18, 2016); Esme Nicholson, "'Migrant Hire' Connects Refugees to German Tech Industry," *NPR* (February 10, 2017); Hussein Shaker, "Why I Want to Help 10,000 Refugees Get Jobs," *The Eureka.com* (April 16, 2016).
20. Michael Bleby, Caitlin Fitzsimmons and Nassim Khadem, "We came by boat – how refugees changed Australian business," *The Sydney Morning Herald* (September 10, 2013); Tan Le, "My Immigration Story," (December 2011); Max Walden, "Australia's 'Boat People': Then and Now," *The Diplomat* (June 21, 2016).
21. Susan F. Martin, "Rethinking Protection of Those Displaced by Humanitarian Crises," *American Economic Review*, vol. 106, no. 5 (2016), pp. 446–450; United Nations High Commissioner for Refugees (UNHCR), *Global Trends: Forced Displacement in 2015* (Geneva, Switzerland: UNHCR, 2015).
22. Anouch Missirian and Wolfram Schlenker, "Asylum applications and migration flows," *American Economic Review*, vol. 107, no. 5 (2017), pp. 436–440; Daniela Wech, "Asylum Applicants in the EU—An Overview," *CESifo DICE*, vol. 14, no. 3 (2016), pp. 59–64.
23. Eva Degler and Thomas Liebig, *Finding Their Way: Labour Market Integration of Refugees in Germany* (Paris: OECD, 2017); Victoria M. Esses, Ulrich Wagner, Carina Wolf, Matthias Preiser and Christopher

J. Wilbur, "Perceptions of National Identity and Attitudes Toward Immigrants and Immigration in Canada and Germany," *International Journal of Intercultural Relations*, vol. 30, no. 6 (2006), pp. 653–669; Timothy J. Hatton, "Refugees, Asylum Seekers, and Policy in OECD Countries," *American Economic Review*, vol. 106, no. 5 (2016), pp. 441–445; Peter S. Li, *Destination Canada: Immigration Debates and Issues* (Don Mills, Ontario: Oxford University Press, 2003); Per Lundborg, "Refugees' Employment Integration in Sweden: Cultural Distance and Labor Market Performance," *Review of International Economics*, vol. 21, no. 2 (2013), pp. 219–232.

24. Laurie Monsebraaten, "Income gap persists for recent immigrants, visible minorities and Indigenous Canadians," *The Star* (October 26, 2017); Garnett Picot and Feng Hou, *Immigration, Low Income and Income Inequality in Canada: What's New in the 2000s?* Catalogue no. 11F0019M—No. 364 (Ottawa: Statistics Canada, 2014).

25. Kathryn H. Anderson, "Can Immigrants ever Earn as Much as Native Workers?" *IZA World of Labor*, 159 (2015); George J. Borjas, "Self-Selection and the Earnings of Immigrants," *American Economic Review*, vol. 77, no. 4 (1987), pp. 531–553; William C. Smith and Frank Fernandez, "Education and Wage Gaps: A Comparative Study of Immigrant and Native Employees in the United States and Canada," *American Institutes for Research* (2015).

26. Kathryn H. Anderson (2015); Thomas Y. Mathä, Alessandro Porpiglia and Eva Sierminska, "The Immigrant/Native Wealth Gap in Germany, Italy and Luxembourg," European Central Bank, Working Paper Series No. 1302, Conference on Household Finance and Consumption (2011).

27. Liz Hacken, "Five Questions with Clarence Wooten," *The Baltimore Sun* (October 1, 2009); Jonathan P., Hicks, "Reginald F. Lewis, 50, Is Dead; Financier Led Beatrice Takeover," *New York Times* (January 20, 1993); Jeffrey A. Tannenbaum, "The Racial Ravine," *Wall Street Journal* (May 22, 2000); Devin Thorpe, "Successful African-American Silicon Valley Entrepreneur Feels 'Like A Black Unicorn'," *Forbes* (January 15, 2018).

28. Taehyun Ahn, "Racial Differences in Self-Employment Exits," *Small Business Economics*, vol. 36, no. 2 (2011), pp. 169–186; Timothy Bates, "Minority Entrepreneurship," *Foundations and Trends in Entrepreneurship*, vol. 7, no. 3–4 (2011), pp. 151–311; David G. Blanchflower, "Minority Self-employment in the United States and the Impact of Affirmative Action Programs," *Annals of Finance*, vol. 5, no. 3–4 (2009), 361–396; Raj Chetty, Nathaniel Hendren, Maggie R. Jones and Sonya R. Porter, "Race and Economic Opportunity in the United States: An Intergenerational Perspective," NBER Working Paper No. 24441 (March 2018); Linda F. Edelman, Candida G. Brush, Tatiana S. Manolova, and Patricia G. Greene, "Start-up Motivations and Growth Intentions of Minority

Nascent Entrepreneurs," *Journal of Small Business Management*, vol. 48, no. 2 (2010), pp. 174–196; Robert W. Fairlie and Alicia M. Robb, "Why Are Black Owned Businesses Less Successful than White Owned Businesses? The Role of Families, Inheritances, and Business Human Capital," *Journal of Labor Economics*, vol. 25, no. 2 (2007), pp. 289–323; Robert W. Fairlie and Alicia M. Robb, *Race and Entrepreneurial Success: Black-, Asian-, and White-Owned Businesses in the United States* (Cambridge: The MIT Press, 2008); Philipp Köllinger and Maria Minniti, "Not for Lack of Trying: American Entrepreneurship in Black and White," *Small Business Economics*, vol. 27, no. 1 (2006), pp. 59–79.

29. Hernando de Soto, *The Mystery of Capital: Why Capitalism Triumphs in the West and Fails Everywhere Else* (New York: Basic Books, 2000).

30. Daniel Córdova, "Defeating Poverty Doing Business: The Case of the Flores Family and Topy Top," in Alvaro Vargas Llosa, ed., *Lessons from the Poor: Triumph of the Entrepreneurial Spirit* (Oakland: The Independent Institute, 2008), pp. 55–120; Matt Moffett, "A Rags-to-Riches Career Highlights Latin Resurgence," *Wall Street Journal* (November 15, 2011).

31. William D. Bygrave and Charles W. Hofer, "Theorising about Entrepreneurship," *Entrepreneurship Theory and Practice*, vol. 16, no. 2 (1991), pp. 13–22; William B. Gartner, "'Who Is an Entrepreneur?' Is the Wrong Question," *Entrepreneurship Theory and Practice*, vol. 13, no. 4 (1989), pp. 47–68.

32. Scott Shane and S. Venkataraman, "The Promise of Entrepreneurship as a Field of Research," *Academy of Management Review*, vol. 25, no. 1 (2000), pp. 217–226.

33. Joern H. Block, Karsten Kohn, Danny Miller and Katrin Ullrich, "Necessity Entrepreneurship and Competitive Strategy," *Small Business Economics*, vol. 44, no. 1 (2015), pp. 37–54; Simon C. Parker, *The Economics of Entrepreneurship* (Cambridge: Cambridge University Press, 2009).

34. Marianne Bertrand and Sendhil Mullainathan, "Are Emily and Greg More Employable Than Lakisha and Jamal? A Field Experiment on Labor Market Discrimination," *American Economic Review*, vol. 94, no. 4 (2004), pp. 991–1013; Philip Oreopoulos, "Why Do Skilled Immigrants Struggle in the Labor Market? A Field Experiment with Thirteen Thousand Resumes," *American Economic Journal: Economic Policy*, vol. 3, no. 4 (2011), pp. 148–171.

35. I have recounted Bimpe Nkontchou's story based on the following sources: Lakshmi Ramarajan and Emily LeRoux-Rutledge, "How Identities and Discrimination Catalyze Global Entrepreneurship," in Laura Morgan Roberts, Lynn Perry Wooten and Martin N. Davidson, eds., *Positive Organizing in a Global Society: Understanding and Engaging: Understanding and Engaging Differences for Capacity Building & Inclusion* (New York:

Routledge, 2016), pp. 37–42; and social media—i.e., LinkedIn account: https://www.linkedin.com/in/bimpe-nkontchou-ba741a4/ (Accessed 30 November 2018).
36. Ramarajan and LeRoux-Rutledge (2016, p. 37).
37. For more comprehensive accounts on necessity entrepreneurship, and other relevant aspects of black, Asian, ethnic minority (BAME) entrepreneurs and their ventures, see the following sources: Giles A. Barrett, Trevor P. Jones and David McEvoy, "Socio-economic and Policy Dimensions of the Mixed Embeddedness of Ethnic Minority Business in Britain," *Journal of Ethnic and Migration Studies*, vol. 27, no. 2 (2001), pp. 241–258; Sara Carter, Samuel Mwaura, Monder Ram, Kiran Trehan and Trevor Jones, "Barriers to Ethnic Minority and Women's Enterprise: Existing Evidence, Policy Tensions and Unsettled Questions," *International Small Business Journal*, vol. 33, no. 1 (2015), pp. 49–69; Ken Clark and Stephen Drinkwater, "Recent Trends in Minority Ethnic Entrepreneurship in Britain," *International Small Business Journal*, vol. 28, no. 2 (2010), pp. 136–146; Mohammed Ishaq, Asifa Hussain and Geoff Whittam "Racism: A Barrier to Entry? Experiences of Small Ethnic Minority Retail Businesses," *International Small Business Journal*, vol. 28, no. 4 (2010), pp. 362–377; Monder Ram and Trevor Jones, *Ethnic Minorities in Business* (Milton Keynes: The Small Enterprise Research Team, Open University, 2008); Monder Ram, Trevor Jones, Paul Edwards, Alexander Kiselinchev, Lovemore Muchenje and Kassa Woldesenbet, "Engaging with Super-Diversity: New Migrant Businesses and the Research–Policy Nexus," *International Small Business Journal*, vol. 31, no. 4 (2013), pp. 337–356.
38. Parker (2009).
39. Elie Chrysostome, E. (2010). "The Success Factors of Necessity Immigrant Entrepreneurs: In Search of a Model," *Thunderbird International Business Review*, vol. 52, no. 2 (2010), pp. 137–152; Jock Collins, Katherine Watson and Branka Krivokapic-Skoko, *From Boats to Businesses: The Remarkable Journey of Hazara Refugee Entrepreneurs in Adelaide* (Sydney: Centre for Business and Social Innovation, UTS Business School, 2017); Sari Pekkala Kerr and William R. Kerr, "Immigrant Entrepreneurship," in John Haltiwanger, Erik Hurst, Javier Miranda and Antoinette Schoar, eds., *Measuring Entrepreneurial Businesses: Current Knowledge and Challenges* (Chicago: Chicago University Press, 2017), pp. 187–249; Horatio M. Morgan, Sui Sui and Mathias Baum, "Are SMEs with Immigrant Owners Exceptional Exporters?" *Journal of Business Venturing*, vol. 33, no. 3 (2018), pp. 241–260.

PART I

The Outsider Problem

CHAPTER 2

Being on the Outside of Powerful Mainstream Networks

The employees of Alibaba were gathered in a conference room at a hotel in Hangzhou, the capital of Zhejiang province in East China.[1] The year 2003 had arrived, and the night skies were becoming dull as fireworks and celebrations faded in the streets. Still holding on to their confetti and horns, they were patiently waiting because they wanted to know whether they would keep their jobs.

Two years earlier, many e-commerce companies had failed in the United States, leaving a thick cloud of doubt over Alibaba's future. Will it survive as an online business-to-business (B2B) platform that connects many small buyers and sellers in China? Everyone wanted to hear what its co-founder and CEO, Jack Ma, had seen when he looked into future.

As Jack entered the room, the discordant chattering abruptly ended as everyone took their seat. He was wearing a black vest over a yellow-looking long-sleeved, collared shirt tucked into his pants. Standing tall and straight, he held up his chin and looked squarely into a galaxy of eyes fixed on him from below:

> "Starting in 1995 with China pages, and since we founded Alibaba in March 1999, everyone has been saying Alibaba doesn't know how to make money, that Alibaba only knows how to burn money. Last evening at 6 o'clock sharp, we received data which shows Alibaba has become fully profitable. It means as of yesterday, we have made not only 1 yuan, but 500,000 yuan profit," declared Jack, in the manner of a reinvigorated politician seeking re-election after being weighed down by low poll numbers.[2]

A once tamed group broke into a stirring round of applause. Some blew their horns and threw confetti across the room. Then almost everyone took to the floor, dancing and chanting with yellow scarfs around their necks. As they swayed and waved flags in tandem, they belted out songs in unison: "If you don't go through a storm, you'll never see a rainbow. No one can achieve success without a hard effort."[3]

Jack's speech hinted at burdens he had been carrying up to that very night. What else might he have shared had he looked deeper and longer into the past? Now in his late thirties, he was far removed from the 12-year-old boy who routinely rode a bicycle to meet and learn from English-speaking foreigners at a local hotel, or near the banks of the West Lake, in Hangzhou. I imagine that he remembered how amazed he was when he traveled to Australia in his early twenties, and learned for the first time that life beyond China could be fulfilling. Jack's fascination with English would later land him in a classroom as an English teacher.

Afterwards, his entrepreneurial spirit and curiosity lured him far beyond the classroom. In 1992, he established the first English-language translation agency in Hangzhou. But after learning about the internet from a friend in Seattle, he shifted his attention to the World Wide Web for business possibilities.

In 1995, he and his wife, Zhang Ying, pooled about 20,000 yuan (or about US$3000) in savings and created China Pages. They initially thought that this new venture would usher in the internet age in China: every young and small business in China could now be listed in an online directory that was accessible to others well beyond their owners' remote villages. This vision didn't materialize as Jack hoped. But he took his early setback better than many might have: "even if I don't succeed, someone will succeed."[4]

In 1999, he teamed up with about 17 friends to pursue a more promising business venture. With about 500,000 yuan (or about US$60,000) in hand, they started Alibaba in Jack's apartment. As a home-grown, B2B online platform, Alibaba would give less established local manufacturers in China a real opportunity to conduct business in a global marketplace long dominated by Western companies.

Dressed in a dark-blue blazer, collared white shirt and khaki pants, Jack rose to his feet and addressed the group in their first strategy meeting:

> Today, we are all here to discuss what we should do in the next 5 to 10 years. So, what will Alibaba become in the future? Since we were working on China Pages, I've always said our competitors are not domestic websites, but over-

seas websites. Our competitors are not in China, but in America's Silicon Valley. So first, we should position Alibaba as a global website… Second, we need to learn the hard working spirit of Silicon Valley. If we go to work at 8 a.m. and go home at 5 p.m., this is not a high-tech company; and Alibaba will never be successful. If we have that kind of 8 a.m. to 5 p.m. spirit, then we should just go and do something else. Americans are strong at hardware and systems. But on information and software, Chinese brains are just as good as theirs… This is the reason we dare to compete with Americans. If we're a good team and know what we want to do, one of us can defeat ten of them.[5]

This would be one of many times the Alibaba team would seek a rallying call from Jack. They had worked out a strategy to take on U.S. e-commence companies. But they needed a lot more money than 500,000 yuan to execute it. Although China's state-owned banks could help, their primary clients were state-owned companies, many of which were overstaffed and money-losing operations.[6] Not only did they need to quickly source capital outside mainland China, they also urgently needed a well-connected senior executive to do so.

Help finally came when the U.S.-educated lawyer, Joe Tsai, joined Alibaba as its chief financial officer. How relieved Jack must have felt when Joe later told him that money was on the way: US$500,000 from a group of angel investors in Hong Kong; roughly US$3 million from Goldman Sachs in the United States, and US$20 million from Softbank in Japan.

It's hard to believe that Jack had forgotten these things when he delivered his rousing speech in a hotel conference room that night. Perhaps, it was sufficient to remind his staff that all the naysayers were wrong about Alibaba's future. At the same time, he had good reason to cautiously celebrate because the Chinese market was too attractive a field for U.S. e-commerce giants to leave it all to Alibaba. "Someday, eBay would come in our direction," Jack contemplated.[7] The only question was whether he would be ready for that day.

Before 2003 ended, he and his team came up with a defensive strategy that involved the Taobao ("searching for treasure") website. This website allowed ordinary people in China to buy, sell or auction consumer items online at no cost. Jack had anticipated that eBay would enter the Chinese markets and try to court the same customers. But having initially enticed them with free access, he thought they would be reluctant to switch to an online auction site like eBay that charges its users. At the same time, eBay was loaded with more cash than Alibaba. Therefore, it could woo Alibaba's customers by offering even more valuable online services at no cost.

But standing in eBay's way was its business model. It had long made money by targeting fee-paying customers—they had to pay to list items for sale and when they carry out a transaction. Thus, even if Meg Whitman, its then-CEO, had crafted a free-access business model for the Chinese market, she knew that eBay's board of directors and shareholders would be reluctant to support such a strategic response to Alibaba. Therefore, she had to consider other strategic moves.

As early as 2002, eBay was poised to make its entry into China. It had already purchased one-third of the shares of EachNet, a leading Shanghai-based online auction company at the time. The anticipated day of battle finally arrived around the third quarter of 2003. At this stage, eBay had gained control over EachNet by paying an additional US$150 million to increase its ownership level to 67 percent. In another calculated move to prevent Alibaba from advertising through major web portals, eBay also purchased exclusive rights to leading sites such as Sina, Sohu, and Netease. Alibaba responded by turning to TV ads and mobile services, knowing that Chinese customers were more likely to be glued to their TVs and cell phones than to the internet.

Meg and her eBay team sought to take the fight over the Chinese market to a new level by investing an additional US$100 million in EachNet's operations around 2005. In an unexpected move, Jack fired back the same year by raising US$1 billion from Yahoo in exchange for an equity stake of 40 percent in Alibaba. Already unfazed by critics of his free-access model, Jack was now even more emboldened to let Chinese customers use his Taobao site at no cost. Still, eBay insisted that customers had to pay to use its trading platform. But many customers responded by choosing Taobao over eBay.

In 2006, eBay waved a white flag. With a broken spirit, it began to withdraw from the Chinese market. Everyone understood that eBay's departure was underway when it turned over eBay EachNet to Tom Online, a joint venture partner.

Six years later, Jack returned to his largest shareholder, Yahoo, to reclaim half of its 40 percent equity stake for US$7.1 billion, now worth more than seven times its value.

Alibaba now stood well beyond the apartment in which Jack first inspired his co-founding team: "we can beat government agencies and big famous companies because of innovative spirit."[8] What those in the apartment had come to believe in 1999, the world would slowly learn: a small e-commerce operator like Alibaba could indeed prevail over mighty e-commerce giants across the Pacific Ocean.

* * *

Jack Ma's story works nicely as a David-Goliath tale: his fledging Alibaba confronts and prevails over Meg's mighty eBay. But behind this riveting battle on the corporate high seas lie more profound insights. As interesting and unique the details of Jack's story seem, it embodies common difficult challenges that innovative entrepreneurs from diverse marginalized and minority groups are likely to face.

As we look at these difficulties we can think of ourselves as medical doctors diagnosing a condition that I'd like to call the *outsider problem*. In general terms, this problem involves situations in which individuals are primarily disadvantaged because they are outside networks that facilitate superior learning and performance outcomes.[9]

What if I told you that the signs—or objective evidence—that point to the outsider problem in marginalized and minority entrepreneurs are (a) weak or non-existent connections to powerful mainstream networks, (b) lack of relevant know-how, and (c) exposure to stereotype-driven discrimination and stereotype threat.

But knowing the signs of the problem raises a number of further questions: Why and how are marginalized and minority entrepreneurs weakly connected, or unconnected to such networks? Why do they lack relevant know-how? Why and how do stereotypes hurt them?

Let's take on the network-related questions now, and leave the other interesting ones for later.

Whether you live in a rich or poor country, you will find that social networks matter for your survival and success. After all, we're all faced with the basic challenge of earning a living in an increasingly competitive and globalized knowledge-based economy. In practice, this means we have to find clever ways to innovate and create value based on what we know. Doing so essentially comes down to whether we know how to make existing things better, or create new things—such as products, services, information solutions, or organizational forms—for which people are willing to pay more than they cost in terms of time, energy and money. At the same time, the most valuable knowledge is often created and shared among people who already know and trust each other. Therefore, we also need to have access to critical networks in mainstream society to get ahead in general, and particularly in the global marketplace.[10]

The influence of networks is far-reaching. Oftentimes, what or who counts in the world and organizations as the "leader," "best practice," "exemplary," "pioneering," "authority," or "iconic" is not necessarily what or who is demonstrably most capable, efficient or effective. Many times it comes down to what, or whom, well-networked and traditionally dominant groups endorse as socially acceptable or legitimate.[11] Such endorsements are very important because they facilitate access to powerful actors and critical resources, and promote conformance with mainstream ideas, practices or behaviors.[12]

A common setback for minority entrepreneurs is that their network, or web of interpersonal relationships, is underdeveloped and under-resourced. One reason for this is that they generally lack access to well-connected and highly successful individuals from traditionally dominant groups in mainstream society. This also means that they miss out on the learning- and performance-enhancing benefits that powerful mainstream networks exclusively offer to their members.

Research indicates that black and Hispanic professionals are held back by network-related challenges that carry over from the job market or workplace to entrepreneurship. Specifically, they often struggle to land and retain senior management jobs because they lack vital connections within their organization and the larger industry.[13] The lack of such connections also hampers them as entrepreneurs.[14] For example, they are less likely than others to get the kind of advice they need to build and grow new ventures into global companies with reputable brands. Such advice spans opinions or information on lots of things, including business ideas that are most promising, management of intellectual property, recruitment of high-potential employees, pitching to private equity investors (i.e., business angels or venture capital funds), negotiation with suppliers, or best practices in customer service.

Furthermore, since entrepreneurs generally need to go outside their circle of family members and friends when seeking funds to scale up their ventures,[15] the lack of mainstream connections could mean that marginalized and minority entrepreneurs will be especially disadvantaged when dealing with mainstream players such as private equity investors.[16]

When Clarence was working on the ImageCafe venture in 1998, he entered a partnership with MindSpring, an established internet service provider. Under this partnership, MindSpring business customers were able to download ImageCafe's webpage templates through MindSpring.com. In addition to increasing ImageCafe's revenue-generating potential, this partnership helped Clarence by signaling to potential investors that he was a vetted and credible high-tech entrepreneur.[17] It also signaled that he had a promising, though hardly unique, business model at the time. However, he later struggled to raise a sufficiently large amount of capital from private equity investors. Faced with an offer of US$23 million from Network Solutions/Verisign for the business, he and his partners decided to prematurely exit with cash rather than continue.

When one considers how business angels and venture capital funds make funding decisions, it's not hard to see why Clarence and other minority entrepreneurs are unlikely to receive substantial funding, if any, from them. These private equity investors favor entrepreneurs with extensive industry experience, highly demanded products, and businesses that can be rapidly scaled up at a low cost.[18] They are also inclined to conduct business with entrepreneurs whom they personally know and trust, or who have been referred to them by their trusted industry partners.[19]

More generally, the players that dominate mainstream networks are inclined to overlook minority entrepreneurs because of the emphasis they place on pre-existing friendship and trust when conducting business. This message comes through clearly from Reid Hoffman, the founder of LinkedIn: "… the only times that I work with people are when someone comes strongly recommended to me through a source that I trust," he once said.[20]

Perhaps Clarence might have found it difficult to initiate business with Reid if none of his personal contacts knew him very well. But suppose he had just met someone who happens to be Reid's long-time friend. Let's call this person Peter. Although Clarence has found a mutual acquaintance, his chance of getting through to Reid might still be small because Peter may be reluctant to strongly endorse him. He might be unwilling to do so because he could be putting his reputation and friendship with Reid on the line—for instance, if a deal between Clarence and Reid were to turn sour, Peter could fall outside Reid's small circle of trust. In other words, I imagine that Peter understands that Reid trusts his ability to judge character; and therefore, will be selective when endorsing new contacts.

To be fair to Reid, it makes sense for people to do business with other people they already know and trust. As it turns out, this preference is consistent with normal social dynamics that promote a pattern of networking and relationship building that work against minority entrepreneurs. Two notable social dynamics come to mind. First, people with similar backgrounds (e.g., race, class, gender, and/or education) are more likely to form personal and professional relationships with each other.[21] And second, people prefer to form new relationships with people who are already well connected.[22]

When these two social dynamics combine, we end up with a situation in which an elite group of players achieve and maintain dominant positions in resource-rich and high-status networks in mainstream society. For example, we observe this episode in Silicon Valley, where white male business leaders have long dominated the entrepreneurial and innovation ecosystems, virtually leaving racialized professionals and entrepreneurs—especially blacks and Hispanics—on the fringes of these ecosystems.[23]

Entrepreneurs from marginalized and minority groups may respond to social isolation in mainstream society by forming their own informal and formal networks. In fact, they often do so. However, research suggests that such networks are usually small and dominated by family members and friends.[24] Minority entrepreneurs may primarily turn to such cohesive networks for psychosocial support because they provide a safe space for discussing personal or sensitive issues. They may also cultivate bonds of trust or solidarity, and feel a sense of self-worth and belonging in these networks. In addition, they can learn coping strategies from their trusted contacts too.

Although support networks along these lines can be helpful, they often fall short of mainstream networks in ways that preclude them from delivering the kinds of learning- and performance-enhancing benefits that marginalized and minority entrepreneurs really need.[25] In particular, newly formed marginalized- or minority-only networks (i.e., immigrant-, women-, black-, Hispanic-, or Asian-only associations) are unlikely to be a major source of novel and advantageous information because diversity of thought or perspectives is often sacrificed for solidarity.

This could mean that much of what marginalized and minority entrepreneurs learn from their tightly knit circle of family, friends and business associates is redundant information. In other words, these networks could be echo chambers that reinforce their pre-existing core beliefs, ideas, values or expectations. On the contrary, although they might receive less psychosocial benefits from larger and more diverse mainstream networks, they can significantly benefit from the novel information that predominantly flow from weak social ties or acquaintances.[26] These weak social ties are key sources of innovation-enabling novel information because their ideas, lived experiences, beliefs and expectations are often fundamentally different from those of entrepreneurs from marginalized and minority groups.

Formal marginalized- or minority-only networks, such as fee-based professional and business associations, also have shortcomings that must be weighed against their expected benefits. The larger these networks are, the greater their actual and perceived benefits will be; and hence, the greater their chance of attracting new members. However, the initial motivations, goals, support and solidarity that helped create these formal networks can constrain their growth potential. In addition, the compromises that are required to foster network growth can trigger tension and conflict among network leaders and members.

For example, perhaps more established minority entrepreneurs with limited time to network might only consider minority-only business associations when they provide valuable business-related benefits (e.g., sales leads, mentoring, endorsement or sponsorship, strategic advice, access to industry leaders); and/or when they have the potential to significantly grow in size and especially status. At the same time, some founding or less established members in such business associations might become disgruntled if they were forced to depart from the initial goals, values or traditional ways of doing things. This sets the stage for divergent expectations and interpersonal conflicts between more and less established members, or between new members and older ones. If poorly managed, these conflicts could leave everyone unsatisfied. This could put the very survival of a minority-only business association at risk.

In sum, we have a case where marginalized and minority entrepreneurs lack access to powerful mainstream networks. Consequently, they come up short on advantageous social capital; that is, the "the sum of the actual and potential resources embedded within, available through, and derived from [their] network of relationships."[27] As will be seen in greater detail later, all entrepreneurs need social capital to develop and grow their ventures.[28] Therefore, social capital deficiency is a major setback for entrepreneurs from marginalized and minority groups. To make things worse, they struggle to develop alternative networks that compensate for this deficiency.

Taken together, these observations reinforce the view that their limited access, if any, to powerful mainstream networks is a key manifestation of the outsider problem that holds them back.

Notes

1. This account is not meant to serve as a biography. I have tried to recreate the events, places, settings, personal characteristics and conversations based on publicly available information, including: Duncan Clarke, *Alibaba: The House That Jack Ma Built* (New York: Ecco, an imprint of HarperCollins Publishers, 2016); Bruce Einhorn, "How eBay Found a Secret Way into China," *Bloomberg* (April 14, 2011); Porter Erisman, *Alibaba's World: How a Remarkable Chinese Company Is Changing the Face of Global Business* (New York: St. Martin's Press, 2015); Rebecca Fannin, "How I Did It: Jack Ma, Alibaba.com," *Inc.com* (January 1, 2008); Liu Shiying and Martha Avery, *Alibaba: The Inside Story Behind Jack Ma and the Creation of the World's Biggest Online Marketplace* (New York: Collins Business, an imprint of HarperCollins Publishers, 2009); Nathan Vanderklippe, "How Goldman Sachs Won and Lost with China's Alibaba," *The Globe and Mail* (March 25, 2017); Helen H. Wang, "How EBay Failed in China," *Forbes* (September 12, 2010); "EBay to Buy Remainder of China's EachNet," *The Wall Street Journal* (June 12, 2003); "Jack Ma Talkasia Transcript," *CNN* (April 25, 2006); "Alibaba Buys Back Stake Held by Yahoo for US$7.1-billion," *Financial Post* (May 21, 2012); "The Jack Who Would Be King," *The Economist* (August 24, 2000).
2. Primary source of quote: "The Alibaba Story – Crocodile in the Yangtze" Film (2014), written and directed by Porter Erisman.
3. Ibid.
4. Ibid.
5. Ibid.
6. Franklin Allen, Jun Qian and Meijun Qian, "Law, Finance, and Economic Growth in China," *Journal of Financial Economics*, vol. 77, no. 1 (2005), pp. 57–116; János Kornai, "The Soft Budget Constraint," *Kyklos*, vol. 39, no. 1 (1986), pp. 3–30.
7. Source of quote: "The Alibaba Story – Crocodile in the Yangtze" Film (2014).
8. Ibid.
9. This characterization of the outsider problem primarily draws on the following work: Jan Johanson and Jan-Erik Vahlne, "The Uppsala Internationalization Process Model Revisited: From Liability of Foreignness to Liability of Outsidership," *Journal of International Business Studies*, vol. 40, no. 9 (2009), pp. 1411–1431. In this study, the authors suggest that a

company's chance of succeeding in foreign markets is relatively low when it is disadvantaged by the "liability of outsidership," as reflected in a diminished potential to learn and develop its capabilities in such markets.
10. Peter L. Berger and Thomas Luckmann, *The Social Construction of Reality: A Treatise in the Sociology of Knowledge* (New York: Doubleday & Company, 1966); Ronald S. Burt, *Structural Holes: The Social Structure of Competition* (Cambridge, MA: Harvard University Press, 1992); Mark Granovetter, "Economic Action and Social Structure: The Problem of Embeddedness," *American Journal of Sociology*, vol. 91, no. 3 (1985), pp. 481–510; Paul DiMaggio and Filiz Garip, "Network Effects and Social Inequality," *Annual Review of Sociology*, vol. 38 (2012), pp. 93–118; Paul J. DiMaggio and Walter W. Powell, "The Iron Cage Revisited: Institutional Isomorphism and Collective Rationality in Organizational Fields," *American Sociological Review*, vol. 48, no. 2 (1983), pp. 147–160.
11. Howard E. Aldrich and C. Marlene Fiol, "Fools Rush in? The Institutional Context of Industry Creation," *Academy of Management Review*, vol. 19, no. 4 (1994), pp. 645–670; Stephanie A. Fernhaber and Patricia P. McDougall-Covin, "Venture Capitalists as Catalysts to New Venture Internationalization: The Impact of Their Knowledge and Reputation Resources, Entrepreneurship Theory and Practice," vol. 33, no. 1 (2009), pp. 277–295; Srilata Zaheer, "Overcoming the Liability of Foreignness," *Academy of Management Journal*, vol. 38, no. 2 (1995), pp. 341–363; Monica A. Zimmerman and Gerald J. Zeitz, "Beyond Survival: Achieving New Venture Growth by Building Legitimacy," *Academy of Management Review*, vol. 27, no. 3 (2002), pp. 414–431; Sze-Sze Wong and Wai Fong Boh, "Leveraging the Ties of Others to Build a Reputation for Trustworthiness Among Peers," *Academy of Management Journal*, vol. 53, no. 1 (2010), pp. 129–148.
12. Ibid.
13. Taehyun Ahn, "Racial Differences in Self-Employment Exits," *Small Business Economics*, vol. 36, no. 2 (2011), pp. 169–186.
14. Ibid.
15. Reddi Kotha and Gerard George, "Friends, Family, or Fools: Entrepreneur Experience and Its Implications for Equity Distribution and Resource Mobilization," *Journal of Business Venturing*, vol. 27, no. 5 (2012), pp. 525–543; Tom Elfring and Willem Hulsink, "Networking by Entrepreneurs: Patterns of Tie—Formation in Emerging Organizations," *Organization Studies*, vol. 28, no. 12 (2016), pp. 1849–1872.
16. Lakshmi Balachandra, Tony Briggs, Kim Eddleston, and Candida Brush, "Don't Pitch Like a Girl!: How Gender Stereotypes Influence Investor Decisions," *Entrepreneurship Theory and Practice*, vol. 43, no. 1 (2019), pp. 116–137.

17. Tannenbaum (2000).
18. Cécile Carpentier and Jean-Marc Suret, "Angel Group Members' Decision Process and Rejection Criteria: A Longitudinal Analysis," *Journal of Business Venturing*, vol. 30, no. 6 (2015), pp. 808–821.
19. Markku Maula, Erkko Autio and Pia Arenius, "What Drives Micro-Angel Investments," *Small Business Economics*, vol. 25, no. 5 (2005), pp. 459–475; Andrew L. Maxwell and Moren Lévesque, "Trustworthiness: A Critical Ingredient for Entrepreneurs Seeking Investors," *Entrepreneurship Theory and Practice*, vol. 38, no. 5 (2014), pp. 1057–1080; Scott Shane and Daniel Cable, "Network Ties, Reputation, and the Financing of New Ventures," *Management Science*, vol. 48, no. 3 (2002), pp. 364–381.
20. Amy Wilkinson, *The Creator's Code* (New York: Simon and Schuster, 2015, pp. 181–182).
21. Miller McPherson, Lynn Smith-Lovin and James M Cook, "Birds of a Feather: Homophily in Social Networks," *Annual Review of Sociology*, vol. 27 (2001), pp. 415–444.
22. Albert-László Barabási, "Scale-Free Networks: A Decade and Beyond," *Science*, vol. 325, no. 5939 (2009), pp. 412–413; Albert-László Barabási and Réka Albert, "Emergence of Scaling in Random Networks," *Science*, vol. 286, no. 5439 (1999): 509–512; Melissa A. Schilling and Christina Fang, "When Hubs Forget, Lie, and Play Favorites: Interpersonal Network Structure, Information Distortion, and Organizational Learning," *Strategic Management Journal*, vol. 35, no. 7 (2014), pp. 974–994.
23. Christopher Mims, "The Age of Tech Superheroes Must End," *The Wall Street Journal* (June 7, 2018); Jay Yarow, "Silicon Valley is 'incredibly white and male' and there's a 'sort of pride' about that fact, says Silicon Valley culture reporter," *Business Insider* (April 4, 2015).
24. Maura McAdam, Richard T. Harrison and Claire M. Leitch, "Stories from the Field: Women's Networking as Gender Capital in Entrepreneurial Ecosystems," *Small Business Economics*, https://doi.org/10.1007/s11187-018-9995-6 (2018), pp. 1–16; Alejandro Portes, Luis Eduardo Guarnizo and William J. Haller, "Transnational Entrepreneurs: An Alternative Form of Immigrant Economic Adaptation," *American Sociological Review*, vol. 67, no. 2 (2002), pp. 278–298; Edward S. Shihadeh and Nicole Flynn, "Segregation and Crime: The Effect of Black Social Isolation on the Rates of Black Urban Violence," *Social Forces*, vol. 74, no. 4 (1996), pp. 1325–1352; Mario Luis Small, "Racial Differences in Networks: Do Neighborhood Conditions Matter?" *Social Science Quarterly*, vol. 88, no. 2 (2007), pp. 320–343; Leann M. Tigges, Irene Browne and Gary P. Green, "Social Isolation of the Urban Poor: Race, Class, and Neighborhood Effects on Social Resources," *Sociological Quarterly*, vol. 39, no. 1 (1998), pp. 53–77.

25. For the related discussion, I draw on insights from the following sources: Marianne Coleman, "Women-Only (Homophilous) Networks Supporting Women Leaders in Education", *Journal of Educational Administration*, vol. 48, no. 6 (2010), pp. 769–781; Herminia Ibarra, "Race, Opportunity, and Diversity of Social Circles in Managerial Networks," *Academy of Management Journal*, vol. 38, no. 3 (1995), pp. 673–703; Herminia Ibarra, "Homophily and Differential Returns: Sex Differences in Network Structure and Access in an Advertising Firm," *Administrative Science Quarterly*, vol. 37, no. 3 (1992), pp. 422–447; Claire M. Leitch, Richard T. Harrison and Frances M. Hill, "Women Entrepreneurs and the Process of Networking as Social Exchange," in Alain Fayolle, Sarah L. Jack, Wadid Lamine and Didier Chabaud, eds., *Entrepreneurial Process and Social Networks: A Dynamic Perspective* (Cheltenham, UK: Edward Elgar, 2016), pp. 157–188; Nan Lin and Mary Dumin, "Access to Occupations through Social Ties," *Social Networks*, vol. 8, no. 4 (1986), pp. 365–385; Gwen Moore, "Structural Determinants of Men's and Women's Personal Networks," *American Sociological Review*, vol. 55, no. 5 (1990), pp. 726–735; Linda A. Renzulli, Howard Aldrich and James Moody, "Family Matters: Gender, Networks, and Entrepreneurial Outcomes," *Social Forces*, vol. 79, no. 2 (2001), pp. 523–546.
26. Granovetter (1973).
27. Janine Nahapiet and Sumantra Ghoshal, "Social Capital, Intellectual Capital, and the Organizational Advantage," *Academy of Management Review*, vol. 23, no. 2 (1998), p. 243.
28. Per Davidsson and Benson Honig, "The Role of Social and Human Capital Among Nascent Entrepreneurs," *Journal of Business Venturing*, vol. 18, no. 3 (2003), pp. 301–331; Eric Gedajlovic, Benson Honig, Curt B. Moore, G. Tyge Payne and Mike Wright, "Social Capital and Entrepreneurship: A Schema and Research Agenda," *Entrepreneurship Theory and Practice*, vol. 37, no. 3 (2013), pp. 455–478; Stam, Wouter, Souren Arzlanian and Tom Elfring, "Social Capital of Entrepreneurs and Small Firm Performance: A Meta-Analysis of Contextual and Methodological Moderators," *Journal of Business Venturing*, vol. 29, no. 1 (2014), pp. 152–173; Brian Uzzi, "Social Structure and Competition in Interfirm Networks: The Paradox of Embeddedness," *Administrative Science Quarterly*, vol. 42, no. 1 (1997), pp. 35–67.

CHAPTER 3

Lacking Relevant Know-How

Like all entrepreneurs, those from marginalized and minority groups will be better positioned to develop thriving ventures when they have practical know-how, as opposed to only textbook concepts or facts. Such know-how or tacit knowledge embodies experience-based and situation-specific knowledge about important entrepreneurial and managerial processes or tasks.[1]

If marginalized and minority entrepreneurs have this kind of know-how, they will know how to do important things that others take for granted, such as: identifying or creating a business idea or opportunity; evaluating its commercial potential; building a founding or top management team with specialized and complementary roles and skills; mobilizing external resources; organizing and coordinating tasks, people, and other resources; inspiring others to work hard and support a vision; converting ideas and resources into novel, or significantly improved, products or services; marketing and selling products or services to target markets; strategizing how to achieve and sustain superior performance; and executing winning strategies. Research suggests that having prior know-how in these areas is indispensable for spotting attractive opportunities, and going on to develop successful ventures, or grow existing companies.[2]

Unfortunately, even with a college or university education, minority entrepreneurs are missing out on the requisite know-how. A key reason for this is that the most effective ways to gain it are largely out of their reach. For example, *learning-by-doing* is a key avenue for gaining such know-how.[3]

This form of learning is based on the observation that people improve at tasks that they repeatedly perform. This is so because each turn at a task provides them with a chance to practice, experiment, and refine their approach after observing the results in different situations. In other words, they will get better results as they accumulate experience because it enables them to appropriately modify and apply their intuitions, and the lessons or rules learnt under different conditions.

When a company adopts a new technology that promises substantial cost-savings, or greater output per employee (i.e., higher labor productivity), the initial results might be disappointing. For instance, operational costs can actually increase because the company has to commit substantial financial resources to cover the cost of installing the new technology and training employees to use it; and productivity might initially fall because employees lack practical knowledge of how to effectively use it.[4] However, the results will improve as they repeatedly use the technology. They will progressively realize its full potential as they identify and fix bugs, experiment with its features or applications, and rearrange how people work, among other things.

In addition to helping employees create greater value for their employers,[5] on-the-job training and learning-by-doing can also provide valuable know-how that comes into play when they start their own business.[6] Professionals from marginalized groups especially need this kind of work experience. Although their ventures have a relatively low chance of survival, research suggests that the results could be better if marginalized and minority entrepreneurs first gain relevant experience by working in established companies before venturing out on their own.[7]

Prior work experience is particularly important in the case of recent foreign-born individuals (i.e., immigrants, migrants or refugees).[8] As newcomers, they are less familiar with their newly adopted host countries (such as the United States, Canada, the United Kingdom, Australia or Germany) than their native-born peers in general; and especially when they originate from countries that significantly differ from their host countries in terms of laws, regulations, standards, values and norms. Even when they pursue formal education in their host countries after arrival, they will still lack the practical knowledge required to effectively adapt to their new business environment.

If they try to learn on their own while launching their ventures, they are likely to make costly mistakes by unwittingly violating informal business conventions or best practices. For example, since they lack prior experience dealing with financial institutions and local investors in their host countries, they might inadvertently turn them away by not following unwritten rules about how to write a proper business plan or pitch ideas. In addition, having not previously served customers in their new adopted countries, they might struggle to grow their customer base because their approach to marketing and sales runs afoul local business norms. As foreign-born entrepreneurs try to develop their ventures, such missteps can rapidly accumulate in different areas; and ultimately, bring down the business.

Returning to Clarence,[9] the African-American serial technology entrepreneur, we can see that entrepreneurs from minority groups needlessly struggle because they come to their ventures with limited prior work experience, if any, as senior executives in leading global corporations. Clarence started out without this kind of experience when he sought to develop ImageCafe venture in 1998. This means that he was particularly disadvantaged because he came to his venture without a sufficiently deep and broad base of practical knowledge that spans critical entrepreneurial and management tasks or processes. As a result, the task of growing and developing his ventures was particularly difficult for him.

The emerging picture is that the initial labor market woes of entrepreneurs from marginalized and minority groups are far more detrimental than previously recognized. It is worth reiterating that if immigrants, blacks, Hispanics, women and other marginalized professionals struggle to find acceptable work, or get promoted to senior management roles, they will be denied on-the-job, learning-by-doing opportunities. Consequently, they will find it difficult to acquire the relevant know-how they need to develop and grow their ventures. Furthermore, limited work experience in the mainstream corporate world might also reinforce their outsider status; and therefore, accentuate gaps in their know-how by virtue of the relatively few opportunities they have to learn from experts.

This brings us to another important way of gaining valuable know-how that is outside the reach of entrepreneurs from marginalized and minority groups: learning from others in mainstream networks. When aspiring entrepreneurs initially work for established corporations, they have the potential to access a boundary-spanning network of co-workers, customers, suppliers, competitors, among others. Research indicates that such organizational networks can facilitate knowledge acquisition and performance-enhancing learning.[10] Although tacit knowledge, or experience-based know-how, is difficult to put into words or writing and share, organizational networks can yield these benefits because they make it possible for individuals to learn from others by engaging in repeated, intensive, face-to-face interactions.[11] They may do so by directly observing how experts within organizational networks perform certain tasks in different contexts, ask questions when things are unclear, and imitate and progressively refine observed practices as they receive feedback.

More generally, organizational networks can facilitate the transfer of valuable tacit knowledge to aspiring entrepreneurs by fostering intensive and trusted interpersonal relationships. These relationships can provide important contextual information or clues. As a result, they will make it easier for aspiring entrepreneurs to identify, assimilate and apply valuable know-how that embodies the situation-specific experience, or intuitions, of top performers in organizational networks.[12]

The challenges of learning within or from mainstream organizational networks are also evident in the case of women entrepreneurs. They come to their ventures with less practical know-how than their white-male peers because they have had fewer opportunities to accumulate practical knowledge and hone their managerial skills through on-the-job learning-by-doing.[13] As previously discussed, professional women still struggle to land senior management roles in Fortune 500 companies[14]; and the few who rise to the top of such companies often leave too soon.[15] This also means that they have relatively few opportunities to learn from top performers in leading organizations or networks. Based on what we already know about female-ethnic-minority business leaders, such as Indra Nooyi, female-ethnic-minority entrepreneurs are likely to be particularly disadvantaged when it comes to acquiring valuable know-how from mainstream organizational networks.

In sum, aspiring marginalized and minority entrepreneurs' inability to effectively access and use key learning channels—that is, on-the-job learning-by-doing and interpersonal learning in mainstream networks—to acquire relevant know-how is another manifestation of the serious nature of the outsider problem.[16]

NOTES

1. This observation builds on insights from the following studies: Dorothy Leonard and Sylvia Sensiper, "The Role of Tacit Knowledge in Group Innovation," *California Management Review*, vol. 40, no. 3 (1998), pp. 112–132; Ikujiro Nonaka, "A Dynamic Theory of Organization

Knowledge Creation," *Organization Science*, vol. 5, no. 1 (1994), pp. 14–37; Michael Polanyi, *The Tacit Dimension* (London: Routledge & Kegan Paul, 1966); Jerry L. Wellman, *Organizational Learning: How Companies and Institutions Manage and Apply Knowledge* (New York: Palgrave Macmillan, 2009).
2. Arnold C. Cooper, "Strategic Management: New Ventures and Small Business," *Long Range Planning*, vol. 14, no. 5 (1981), pp. 39–45; Frédéric Delmar and Scott Shane, "Does Business Planning Facilitate the Development of New Ventures?" *Strategic Management Journal*, vol. 24, no. 12 (2003), pp. 1165–1185; Frédéric Delmar and Scott Shane, "Does Experience Matter? The Effect of Founding Team Experience on the Survival and Sales of Newly Founded Ventures," *Strategic Organization*, vol. 4, no. 3, pp. 215–247; Robert Demir, Karl Wennberg, Alexander McKelvie, "The Strategic Management of High-Growth Firms: A Review and Theoretical Conceptualization," *Long Range Planning*, vol. 50, no. 4 (2017), pp. 431–456; Scott Shane, "Prior Knowledge and the Discovery of Entrepreneurial Opportunities," *Organization Science*, vol. 11, no. 4 (2000), pp. 367–472.
3. This discussion draws on insights from the following sources: Florian Groene and Deepti Nene, *Experience Matters: The Five Commandments of Digital Product Management* (PwC: New York, 2017); Peter Thompson, "How Much Did the Liberty Shipbuilders Learn? New Evidence for an Old Case Study," *Journal of Political Economy*, vol. 109, no. 1 (2001), pp. 103–137; Rebecca Achee Thornton and Peter Thompson, "Learning from Experience and Learning from Others: An Exploration of Learning and Spillovers in Wartime Shipbuilding," *American Economic Review*, vol. 91, no. 5 (2001), pp. 1350–1368.
4. Horatio M. Morgan and Ojelanki Ngwenyama, "Real Options, Learning Cost and Timing Software Upgrades: Towards an Integrative Model for Enterprise Software Upgrade Decision Analysis," *International Journal of Production Economics*, vol. 168 (2015), pp. 211–223.
5. Andries De Grip, "Economic Perspectives of Workplace Learning," In Wim J. Nijhof and Loek F. M. Nieuwenhuis, eds., *The Learning Potential of the Workplace* (Rotterdam, Netherlands: Sense Publishers, 2008), pp. 15–29; Sherwin Rosen, "Learning and Experience in the Labour Market," *Journal of Human Resources*, vol. 7, no. 3 (1972), pp. 326–342.
6. Rajshree Agarwal and Sonali K. Shah, "Knowledge Sources of Entrepreneurship: Firm Formation by Academic, User and Employee Innovators," Research Policy, vol. 43, no. 7 (2014), pp. 1109–1133; Howard E. Aldrich and Tiantian Yang, "How Do Entrepreneurs Know What to Do? Learning and Organizing in New Ventures," *Journal of*

Evolutionary Economics, vol. 24, no. 1 (2014), pp. 59–82; M. Diane Burton, Jesper B. Sørensen and Stanislav D. Dobrev, "A Careers Perspective on Entrepreneurship," *Entrepreneurship Theory and Practice*, vol. 40, no. 2 (2016), pp. 237–247; Pontus Braunerhjelm, Ding Ding and Per Thulin, "The Knowledge Spillover Theory of Intrapreneurship," *Small Business Economics*, vol. 51, no. 1 (2018), pp. 1–30; Marco Corsino, Paola Giuri and Salvatore Torrisi, "Technology Spin-Offs: Teamwork, Autonomy, and the Exploitation Of Business Opportunities," *Journal of Technology Transfer* (2018), https://doi.org/10.1007/s10961-018-9669-1; Marc Gruber, Sung Min Kim and Jan Brinckmann, "What Is an Attractive Business Opportunity? An Empirical Study of Opportunity Evaluation Decisions by Technologists, Managers, and Entrepreneurs," *Strategic Entrepreneurship Journal*, vol. 9, no. 3 (2015), pp. 205–225; Thomas J. Holmes and James A. Schmitz, Jr., "A Theory of Entrepreneurship and Its Application to the Study of Business Transfers," *Journal of Political Economy*, vol. 98, no. 2 (1990), pp. 265–294; Davide Hahn, Tommaso Minola and Kimberly A. Eddleston, "How Do Scientists Contribute to the Performance of Innovative Start-ups? An Imprinting Perspective on Open Innovation," *Journal of Management Studies* (2018), https://doi.org/10.1111/joms.12418; Chihmao Hsieh, "Do the Self-Employed More Likely Emerge from Sequential or Parallel Work Experience in Business-Related Functions?" *Entrepreneurship Theory and Practice*, vol. 40, no. 2 (2016), pp. 307–334; Steven Klepper, "Employee Startups in High-Tech Industries," *Industrial and Corporate Change*, vol. 10, no. 3 (2001), pp. 639–674; Steven Klepper and Sally Sleeper, "Entry by Spinoffs," *Management Science*, vol. 51, no. 8 (2005), pp. 1291–1306; Joseph Raffiee and Jie Feng, "Should I Quit My Day Job?: A Hybrid Path to Entrepreneurship," *Academy of Management Journal*, vol. 57, no. 4 (2014), pp. 936–963; Jesper B. Sørensen and Magali A. Fassiotto, "Organizations as Fonts of Entrepreneurship," *Organization Science*, vol. 22, no. 5 (2011), pp. 1121–1367; Jesper B. Sørensen and Amanda J. Sharkey, "Entrepreneurship as a Mobility Process," *American Sociological Review*, vol. 79, no. 2 (2014), pp. 328–349.
7. Timothy Bates, "Minority Entrepreneurship," *Foundations and Trends(R) in Entrepreneurship*, vol. 7, no. 3–4 (2011), pp. 151–311.
8. Natasha Iskander and Nichola Lowe, "Hidden Talent: Tacit Skill Formation and Labor Market Incorporation of Latino Immigrants in the United States," *Journal of Planning Education and Research*, vol. 30, no. 2 (2010), pp. 132–146; José Mata and Claudia Alves, "The Survival of Firms Founded by Immigrants: Institutional Distance between Home and Host Country, and Experience in the Host Country," *Strategic Management Journal*, vol. 39, no. 11 (2018), pp. 2965–2991.
9. Tannenbaum (2000).

10. Paul Almeida and Bruce Kogut, "Localization of Knowledge and the Mobility of Engineers in Regional Networks," *Management Science*, vol. 45, no. 7 (1999), pp. 905–1024; Linda Argote and Erin Fahrenkopf, "Knowledge Transfer in Organizations: The Roles of Members, Tasks, Tools, and Networks," *Organizational Behavior and Human Decision Processes*, vol. 136 (2016), pp. 146–159; Jeffrey H. Dyer and Nile W. Hatch, "Relation-Specific Capabilities and Barriers to Knowledge Transfers: Creating Advantage through Network Relationships," *Strategic Management Journal*, vol. 27, no. 8 (2006), pp. 701–719; Srikanth Paruchuri, "Intraorganizational Networks, Interorganizational Networks, and the Impact of Central Inventors: A Longitudinal Study of Pharmaceutical Firms," *Organization Science*, vol. 21, no. 1 (2010), pp. 1–309.
11. Leonard and Sensiper (1998); Daniel Z. Levin and Rob Cross, "The Strength of Weak Ties You Can Trust: The Mediating Role of Trust in Effective Knowledge Transfer," *Management Science*, vol. 50, no. 11 (2004), pp. 1477–1490; Ramana Nanda and Jesper B. Sørensen, "Workplace Peers and Entrepreneurship," *Management Science*, vol. 56, no. 7 (2010), pp. 1116–1126; Nonaka (1994); Salih Zeki Ozdemir, Peter Moran, Xing Zhong and Martin J. Bliemel, "Reaching and Acquiring Valuable Resources: The Entrepreneur's use of Brokerage, Cohesion, and Embeddedness," *Entrepreneurship Theory and Practice*, vol. 40, no. 1 (2016), pp. 49–79.
12. Anne Domurath and Holger Patzelt, "Entrepreneurs' Assessments of Early International Entry: The Role of Foreign Social Ties, Venture Absorptive Capacity, and Generalized Trust in Others," *Entrepreneurship Theory and Practice*, vol. 40, no. 5 (2016), pp. 1149–1177.
13. Richard J. Boden JR and Alfred R. Nucci, "On the Survival Prospects of Men's and Women's New Business Ventures," *Journal of Business Venturing*, vol. 15, no. 4 (2000), pp. 347–362; Roxanne Zolin, John Watson and Michael Stuetzer, "Challenging the Female Underperformance Hypothesis," *International Journal of Gender and Entrepreneurship*, vol. 5, no. 2 (2013), pp. 116–129.
14. Cook and Glass (2014); Cotter et al. (2001); Gorman and Kmec (2009); Sue (2009).
15. Brescoll et al. (2010); Gupta et al. (2018); Ryan and Haslam (2007).
16. Timothy Bates, William E. Jackson, III and James H. Johnson, Jr., "Introduction: Advancing Research on Minority Entrepreneurship," *Annals of the American Academy of Political and Social Science*, vol. 613, Advancing Research on Minority Entrepreneurship (2007), pp. 10–17; Candida G. Brush, Anne de Bruin, Friederike Welter, "A Gender-Aware Framework for Women's Entrepreneurship," *International Journal of Gender and Entrepreneurship*, vol. 1, no. 1 (2009), pp. 8–24; Carter et al. (2015).

CHAPTER 4

Being Subject to Stereotype-Driven Discrimination and Stereotype Threat

Even when marginalized and minority entrepreneurs are capable and have promising business ideas, discriminatory practices can hold them back. Those who engage in such practices may be motivated by prejudice or negative attitudes. However, a closer look at the underlying issues will show that pervasive negative stereotypes are predominantly at work.

Negative stereotypes are reflected in the unfavorable beliefs, associations, or oversimplified generalizations, that people make about the traits, or social roles, of other groups of people.[1] Since enterprising individuals from minority groups might be disproportionately represented among necessity entrepreneurs, it's particularly important to understand why and how various forms of stereotypical beliefs might impact them as they move between the job market and entrepreneurship.

We can actually learn a lot about stereotypes by looking at what dominant groups believe and say about less established or minority ones.[2] As humans, we engage with individuals or groups with curiosity. Oftentimes, we want answers to questions such as: What does this person (group) want from me (us)? Does this person (group) have what it takes to achieve it? The first question speaks to intent, while the second speaks to capability. Dominant groups are normally able to influence the general perception of other groups' intent and capability in mainstream society. They may do so by stereotyping them. Specifically, they may portray their intent and capability in positive or negative terms, such as "warm" versus "cold," and "competent" versus "incompetent," respectively.

Here is how this works. Dominant groups associate warmth with minority groups that cooperate with them and associate cold with minority groups that they perceive as self-serving or competitors. Meanwhile, they associate competence with high-status minority groups, and incompetence with low-status ones. By stereotyping minority groups in this way, dominant groups can express negative attitudes toward different minority groups in overt or subtle ways.[3]

At one extreme, people from a dominant group, such as white male founder-CEOs in Silicon Valley,[4] may elicit pride and admiration in mainstream society because they are favorably stereotyped as both competent and warm. At the other extreme, people from traditionally disadvantaged groups, such as African-Americans or Hispanics, are treated less favorably. If they are stereotyped as incompetent and cold, they may be subject to prejudice in the form of contempt and disgust from others. Alternatively, they may receive pity from others if they are stereotyped, instead, as incompetent, but warm.

Asians are often portrayed as "too competent, too ambitious, too hardworking, and, simultaneously, not sociable."[5] Based on anti-Semitic-inspired beliefs about Jews' economic success, they are often perceived as competent, but self-serving. So we have a case where Asians and Jews are often subjected to envy or jealousy because they are stereotyped as competent, but cold.

All marginalized groups generally fare worse than the dominant group in terms of their level of exposure to negative stereotypes and prejudice. For example, there is evidence that Harvard University's admission decision-making process is biased against Asian-American applicants with high test scores. This process does so by placing more emphasis on subjective personal ratings on which white American applicants generally score higher—that is, "positive personality," likeability, courage, kindness and being "widely respected."[6]

Traditionally disadvantaged groups, such as African-Americans and Hispanics, are likely to fare even worse because they are often stereotyped as incompetent at critical work- and business-related tasks or activities.[7] Specifically, they may be exposed to stronger negative emotion responses (i.e., anger as opposed to envy), and more discrimination from others in mainstream society. Immigrants, refugees or women may similarly suffer when their competence is called into question.[8]

Given the tendency of dominant groups to hold such stereotypical beliefs, minority entrepreneurs can be particularly disadvantaged when prejudice is also at work. By this I mean, the negative attitudes people hold toward others, or the unfavorable evaluations they make about them. If we were to put such evaluations under a microscope, the key elements that would come to the surface are (a) beliefs that are not based on facts or comprehensive evidence, (b) negative feelings, and (c) tendencies toward unfriendly or hostile behaviors.[9]

For an example, let's return to Aquilino Flores. I wonder how being initially poor might have held him back as an emerging entrepreneur. Imagine he wanted to secure a loan from a mainstream bank in Peru whose manager, Fernandez, *believes* most *poor people* are *lazy, feels disgusted* when he sees them, and tries to *avoid* them as much as possible. Notice the negative and unfounded belief ("poor people are lazy") (what about the hard-working poor?[10]); negative feeling ("... *feels disgusted*...")? And the unfriendly behavior ("tries to avoid them")?

Now, let's assume that Fernandez had spotted Aquilino washing cars in the barrios multiple times before he started Topitop. Imagine that Aquilino had actually gone to the bank and sought loan application information from Fernandez. How helpful do you think Fernandez would have been? Do you see him patiently walking Aquilino through all the available small business loan options at his bank? Would he try to learn about Aquilino's business plan, and make recommendations that were appropriate for his specific needs? I'm not sure about you, but based on Fernandez' negative attitude toward the poor, I'm doubtful that he would have treated Aquilino as well as he might have treated someone else from an upper-class family. It is conceivable that bank managers in advanced Western countries may be less helpful when dealing with entrepreneurs from low-income groups because of prejudicial beliefs.

For an example of a serious case of prejudice, let's return to Jack Ma. By the time he started Alibaba in 1999, China had become a different place than the one he knew as a boy.[11] Once closed to the world, China was becoming more open to large Western multinational corporations and investors as market-oriented reforms—launched by Deng Xiaoping around 1978—took hold. But the Communist Party was still the only game in town. Its tight grip on China's economic and political life had largely remained unchanged. The Party had primarily sought to modernize its historically overstaffed and inefficient state-owned enterprises (SOEs) in strategically important sectors, such as banking, energy, steel, transportation, construction, and telecommunications. It had also sought to specifically transform some SOEs into national champions, with a mandate to become global leaders.

Those who had expected the Party to undertake Western-style privatization were disappointed. There was still limited support for home-grown private companies. In addition, business leaders in government-funded companies had to cautiously operate under the watchful eyes of the Chinese government. After all, they could face serious penalties if arbitrarily accused of economic crimes. This meant that Chinese business leaders had to be mindful of the Party's long-standing view of self-interest as a fatal flaw of Western capitalism.

This is something that Liu Chuanzhi, co-founder of the personal computer maker Lenovo, understands very well: "In order for someone to do well in business in China, he must be concerned about the economy, the politics, and the [political] philosophy," he once said.[12] Before Lenovo, there was the unbranded computer business, Lian Xiang, which Liu and his ten colleagues co-founded in 1984. The Chinese Academy of Sciences contributed about $25,000 toward their start-up capital. This created some challenges for Liu. In addition to going up against Western foreign computer makers that were setting up major operations in China, he had to continuously affirm his loyalty to the Chinese government. This meant complying with its directives as much as possible, and shunning behaviors that the Chinese government might perceive as a self-serving, or a private enterprise approach.

Like other Chinese business leaders, Jack sought to develop Alibaba from a disadvantaged starting point. He had to carefully make his moves because a powerful state actor had automatically relegated him to the undesirable "self-interested" or "Western capitalist" category. Prejudice was behind this: the state didn't establish that Jack was involved in objectively counterproductive or harmful behaviors; instead, it had ascribed sinister motives to him based on his association with a private business operation. This opened the door to state-sponsored discrimination, particularly when it came to financial institutions. Under a state-controlled banking system that favored SOEs over private enterprises,[13] Alibaba's survival was initially on the line because Jack had limited access to finance from banks in China.

Up to this point, we have seen the potential of prejudice and stereotypes to lead to discrimination at levels that hurt minority entrepreneurs. Yet as repulsive as stereotypes and discrimination are, it is possible for both to occur without conscious prejudice at work.[14] No wonder so many managers and executives in charge of hiring workers, or lending money, bristle at the suggestion that they are engaged in discriminatory practices.

For example, if you were to ask a Canadian hiring manager why he called back more Canadian-born applicants than immigrant ones, you are likely to get a reasonable answer along this line:

> [W]hile we were very impressed with Mohammed, Raj and Ying (who happen to be immigrant applicants), we were a bit concerned that their language skills were not as strong as they need to be for the job. That really sucks because we were all excited when we pulled their resumes. They're good candidates. But our company serves clients across Canada, and communication is a big part of what we do. So in the end, we decided to go with Peter and Emily (who happen to be white Canadian-born applicants).[15]

What about a leading American company whose board of directors is considering "John" and "Mary" as potential replacements for an outgoing CEO, "Mark"? If the directors gave the nod to John, you can bet they'll have a good reason for doing so:

> We're lucky to have Mary manage our Latin American division as the vice-president of marketing. Thanks to her, we've maintained a strong position in this region, and expect to generate revenue growth by at least 5 percent next year. We all feel she would serve us well in a CEO role, but these are challenging times in our industry… We decided to go with John based on his substantial experience. Our industry is consolidating, and we'll have to make a few acquisitions over the next 5 years. John was heavily involved in our last two acquisitions. And so far, we're very pleased with the results. In fact, when we announced the last deal, our stock price went up by 25 percent. So for us, it makes sense for John to lead our corporate acquisition strategy.

In these scenarios, the presumption is that the decisions in question were made on the basis of objective criteria. According to the decision makers, all candidates were evaluated on the basis of objective measures of their qualifications—that is, education, professional designations or certifications, work or industry experience, language skills, employment history, and so on. Furthermore, the selection process is presumed to be fair: more qualified individuals were chosen over less qualified ones. Mohammed, Raj and Ying would have received a callback for an interview had their language skills been better than those of Peter and Emily. Similarly, if

Mary had more experience than John, she would have landed the top-manager job. As a result, the unwavering claim is that there is no discrimination at work.

Still, the consequences are real for those who are denied such job and promotion opportunities. As previously suggested, they will miss out on opportunities to earn, and gain relevant know-how. We also know that they might be pushed into entrepreneurship when confronted with disappointing job market and workplace outcomes.[16] After all, this is how we expect necessity entrepreneurs to start their entrepreneurial journey. A major challenge for these entrepreneurs is that the preliminary barriers that pushed them into entrepreneurship might persist in other forms later; and with the same pattern of reasonable justifications from key decision makers linked to subsequent barriers.

Imagine a recent immigrant in Canada decided to start a business after trying to find acceptable work for three years without success. Suppose this immigrant entrepreneur applied for a $25,000 loan without success at Canada's five largest banks—Bank of Montreal (BMO), Bank of Nova Scotia (Scotiabank), Canadian Imperial Bank of Commerce (CIBC), Royal Bank of Canada (RBC), and Toronto–Dominion Bank (TD). Now, assume that several Canadian-born entrepreneurs with a similar business operation were approved on their first submitted loan application for $50,000.

Isn't this an example of how Canadian banks are discriminating against immigrant business owners? Not necessarily. A local branch manager can explain the different loan application outcomes in a reasonable way:

> We don't approve loans at the branches. All loan applications that are submitted at our location are processed by our automated loan approval system in Toronto. Our clients' records are confidential; so I can't discuss the specific cases with you. However, a low credit score is a common reason why banks in Canada, not just us, deny loan applications. In general, immigrant entrepreneurs tend to have a lower credit score than Canadian-born entrepreneurs, and especially when they just arrive. But their score can improve as they build their credit history—by using credit cards and paying their bills on time… We treat all our clients the same.[17]

As before, the impression is that there is nothing to see here. The underlying claim is that borrowers' creditworthiness is evaluated based on objective criteria—that is, a credit score that excludes personal or subjective considerations—and a fair process—that is, entrepreneurs' loan applications are approved when their credit scores exceed a predetermined level.

Suppose we change the country setting from Canada to the United Kingdom, and replace the recent immigrant entrepreneur in the story with an entrepreneur from the black, Asian and minority ethnic (BAME) segment of the population—for example, a black African, black Caribbean, Pakistani, Bangladeshi or Indian entrepreneur. Research suggests that these ethnic-minority entrepreneurs will have higher loan denial rates than their white counterparts.[18] Furthermore, because they expect to be turned down by British banks, they are reluctant to apply for loans in the first place.[19]

But like their Canadian peers, British loan managers would be keen to point out that their banks are objective and fair when evaluating the loan applications of ethnic minorities and whites alike. They can back up this claim with evidence too. For example, there is evidence that the loan denial rate is relatively high for black African business owners and their firms because "more than half of Black African firms (55.7%) [have been found to exceed] their overdraft limit or missed loan repayments versus about 1 in 4 (23.3%) of White firms."[20]

Taking the spotlight off hiring managers and loan officers for a moment, even you could be accused of stereotyping and discrimination when making a basic decision such as purchasing a used car. Like others, you may be suspicious of prices above and below the average range, based on the assumption that all used cars are of roughly equal quality, or equally broken.[21] But if you were to tell all used-car sellers that you will pay only the average price, then you would have effectively stereotyped each seller as an "average seller." In doing so, you would have unintentionally discriminated against above-average or superior sellers. In other words, you would have committed a form of discrimination that economists call *statistical discrimination*.[22]

Statistical discrimination can be at work as marginalized professionals or aspiring entrepreneurs move between the labor market and entrepreneurship. This is likely to occur if employers, banks and others lack the information they need to separate capable individuals from less capable ones when making hiring, promotion, lending decisions, among others. In these situations, decision makers will cautiously proceed by categorizing each person from the marginalized group in question as an "average candidate." While this approach involves stereotyping, it is not motivated by prejudice.

However, against the backdrop of a regrettably long history mired in slavery and racial discrimination,[23] African-American professionals deserve special attention. It is conceivable that they are exposed to discrimination because hiring managers are prejudiced against them. However, the existing evidence does not support the view that conscious prejudice and intentional discrimination are at work; instead, it suggests that hiring managers exhibit unconscious bias that disproportionally work against African-Americans.[24]

This brings us back to the issue of stereotyping. When trying to make sense of whether and why stereotyping and related discriminatory practices are so prevalent, we often overlook apparently ordinary explanations partly because we've been misled by lofty visions of ourselves as rational human beings. We expect each other to make unbiased and sound decisions by conducting comprehensive and time-consuming cost-benefit-style analyses: all alternatives should be carefully considered, and the most rewarding one should be chosen. When people have the information they need, we expect them to reason properly and make sound judgments. When they don't know everything, we expect them to diligently search for information. If their search comes up short, we still expect them to form reasonable expectations about what they don't know. The reality is that we fall short of these and other ideals every day.[25]

We have to come to terms with the observation that stereotyping is a by-product of the way we normally try to cope and function in a complex world. The concept of *heuristics* comes into play here.[26] Heuristics are basically mental short-cuts or simple rules that enable us to simplify and speed up our decision making when there is limited information, time, energy, or money. Such mental short-cuts and simple rules are normally at work in our daily lives because it can be difficult to understand ourselves, others and a complex world. When it comes to relationships, we keep things simple and predictable by predominantly socializing and forming close relationships with people with whom we have similar backgrounds, or lived experiences. We struggle to quickly differentiate between people in meaningful ways; and therefore try to make quick and simple evaluations by putting each other in neat boxes based on superficial and typically observable characteristics (i.e., race or gender). In other words, stereotyping is a common form of heuristics.

Building on the concept of heuristics, cognitive psychologists suggest that how individuals think and act under time pressure or uncertainty can be explained by the interplay between the following two mental processing systems: *system 1*, which facilitates fast, automatic, unconscious, effortless, but error- and bias-prone reasoning, judgments and decisions; and *system 2*, which facilitates slow, deliberate, conscious, mentally demanding, but rational and sound reasoning, judgments and decisions.[27]

In a world rendered difficult and mentally burdensome by time pressure, uncertainty or complexity, system 1 stands out as the default system. Stereotyping and other forms of heuristics are all linked to system 1. If such system-1-driven heuristics are not suppressed, or overridden by system 2, they can lead to errors in our judgments and biased decisions; and consequently, biased and disappointing outcomes.

Similar outcomes can follow when hiring managers and business players automatically or unconsciously adopt a heuristic approach when screening, assessing, selecting or approving others.[28] A major concern is that key mainstream players (i.e., investors, suppliers, or customers) can unconsciously hold negative stereotypes that contribute to unintended discrimination against marginalized and minority entrepreneurs. In doing so, they can inadvertently undermine these entrepreneurs' ability to recognize and exploit attractive business opportunities[29]; and certainly their ability to acquire valuable know-how as they move between the job market and entrepreneurship.

By way of illustration, consider ZintZat.ai., an imaginary Silicon Valley-based start-up.

* * *

ZintZat.ai. has four co-founders—all white males. They have known each other since childhood. With the help of relatives and friends, they pooled their savings and started ZintZat.ai. Its main offerings are software applications that use artificial intelligence (AI) to automatically recognize the personality traits of senior executives based on their unscripted or natural oral and written expressions. These AI-enabled apps need to be fine-tuned, but ZintZat.ai is short-staffed and burning through cash.

Paul, a co-founder and the chief financial officer (CFO), has been reaching out to business angels and venture capital funds to raise capital. When his co-founders suggested that he hire a finance manager to help out, he jumped at the idea. Two days earlier, they had also decided that ZintZat.ai could save money by hiring a freelance software developer rather than another full-time software engineer. Although Rob, the company's chief information officer (CIO), was expected to take care of this latter position, he was scheduled for a surgery that would keep him away from the office for a month.

So Paul took over the whole hiring process. He went around the office, and asked almost everyone to spread the word about the new openings in their networks. But it would take one week before he put together the job descriptions, and post them on the company's website. The following day, the company received 100 applications for both positions. By the time the job postings expired one week later, the number of applications exceeded 1000 in each case.

Around the same time, Paul had started preliminary talks with Chan, an investor in Hong Kong. Chan was interested in purchasing a 10 percent stake in ZintZat.ai for $15 million, and Paul and John (ZintZat.ai's CEO) agreed to meet him in Hong Kong to finalize the deal. They had only one week to prepare for this trip, and needed to a hire a finance manager before they leave. But Paul still hadn't looked at the 1000-plus applications. For the previous three days, they had been working with an accounting firm to estimate the value of the company. They wanted more than $15 million for a 10 percent stake in the business. So they wanted to get the valuation right.

With only two days to go before the Hong Kong trip, Paul finally had a chance to look at the applicants' resumes for the finance manager position during a 30-minute train ride. But just when he was about to scroll to the tenth resume, he received a call from John—who wanted clarification on the three-year growth projection for ZintZat.ai. When the call ended, he had only about ten minutes to get to his second of four scheduled meetings with potential investors in the local area. So he fired off an internal email reminding everyone about the referrals he had requested. With only a day to go before his trip to Hong Kong, another co-founder, James, replied:

> Hey Paul, Sorry I didn't get back to you earlier. But I'd asked one of my buddies, Matt, to apply for the finance position, and I think he did. We attended Wharton together. Those were the best days! He's a finance wiz, but you'd never guess it, because he's one of the coolest guys in the room. He'd definitely be a good fit. By the way, we'll be meeting for a drink later. Most likely at Calave. If you're available around 7 later, we could all meet there. I'll make the introduction. But if you're busy later, I could do so when you return from Hong Kong. Just let me know what works for you. Good luck!

Paul would later meet with James and Matt at Calave. He stayed there much longer than he had planned. As it turned out, Matt was also a friend of his childhood friend, Todd, who had become a leading investment banker at Goldman Sachs. Matt would receive an offer the same night. He accepted it over a handshake and laughter.

When Paul stepped outside Calave that night, he ran into Terrell Grant, who happens to be black. Two years earlier, Terrell was about to complete his master's degree in computer science at the University of Southern California. With only a month to go before graduation, he capitalized on a networking event. It was a symposium on business analytics at the university's main campus grounds. There, he met Paul, who was an invited speaker. They would later run into each other at tech shows, and occasionally at track and field events.

But things were different now. Terrell was now an emerging technology entrepreneur looking for software development projects; and Paul was a senior executive in a sophisticated technology start-up that could use his service on a freelance basis.

"Hey, what are you doing here man?!" said Paul as he reached forward to shake Terrell's hand.
"Wow! Good to see you. I'm actually here to talk business with a colleague," replied Terrell.
"Oh yeah, so what are you working on these days?" asked Paul.
"I'm actually running my own software development company for a year now. It's been a slow start, but I'm trying to land some projects and scale up," replied Terrell.
"Good stuff. We should talk. I'm now leading the finance area at a tech start-up, ZintZat.ai; and we're planning to contract out some of the software development work. So perhaps we could do something on a short-term or freelance basis," stated Paul.
"That would be awesome!" said Terrell.
"Great! Here's my card. Next week I'll be away on business. So touch base with me about two weeks from now, and I'll setup a meeting," replied Paul.

As promised, Paul eventually brought in Terrell to meet the senior executive team at ZintZat.ai. However, things did not work out as well as he had hoped.

Rob had joined the meeting by Skype, about half-way into Terrell's 15-minute presentation on business applications of artificial intelligence in the area of personality trait detection. About two minutes later, Rob interrupted Terrell by asking whether he was familiar with the specific needs of the sophisticated clients that ZintZat.ai intends to serve. Afterwards, Terrell lost his rhythm and confidence. He had previously worried about not being taken seriously as a technology entrepreneur by mainstream business clients. Therefore, he spent a lot of time preparing for this meeting. However, despite his preparation, anxiety took hold of him in ZintZat.ai's boardroom that day.

As his eloquence gave way to virtually inarticulate expressions, Terrell knew that he had missed an opportunity to leave a positive first impression on the senior executive team. Despite a friendly talk with Paul after the meeting, he left without an offer that day; and hasn't received a follow-up call or email since then.

* * *

Taking a step back, let's take a closer look at this hypothetical case. Starting with the first hiring decision, we have a situation where more than 1000 people applied for a finance manager position. In this pile, there were perhaps many qualified immigrant, black, Hispanic, and female candidates, among others. But Paul is a very busy senior executive who's under unrelenting pressure to raise capital, and keep his new venture afloat. At the same time, he needs to process a high volume of applicants under time pressure, but lacks reliable information about them. And even if he had such information, he's unable to diligently review every resume.

By turning to his organizational network for help, he has effectively resorted to a heuristic approach to simplify, and speed up his search and hiring process. This approach basically directs him to prioritize a short list of candidates whom his trusted contacts strongly endorse. This makes sense to Paul because he expects his contacts at ZintZat.ai to recommend only candidates whom they know very well and trust.

However, what starts out as a pragmatic way to fill vacancies under time pressure can be transformed into a conscious, or unconscious, preference for mutually acquainted white males. Given their similar backgrounds or lived experiences, they will be particularly drawn to each other. Furthermore, the more they interact with other, the more likeminded they will become. As a result, they will collectively determine the dominant corporate culture that evolves at ZintZat.ai. This culture can embody stereotypical beliefs that call into question the cultural fit, or competence, of minority job applicants and business partners.

When Terrell met with ZintZat.ai's senior management team that day, he should have been optimistic about his chance of landing a contract to provide software development services. But standing in his way were stereotypical beliefs about black professionals and entrepreneurs that could be activated at any point. Despite his graduate training in computer science, his chance of getting a contract from ZintZat.ai was relatively low because black professionals are likely to be stereotyped as technologically less competent, compared with their white peers.

Terrell's prospects for getting this contract might have been even weaker if one or more of ZintZat.ai's senior executives consciously or unconsciously stereotype individuals from marginalized and minority groups as "poor fit" for their organization. This kind of stereotype would have worked against Terrell because people are susceptible to *confirmation bias*.[30] In this case, this specifically means that some senior executives would be inclined to expect and perceive traits or behaviors in Terrell (i.e., the way he walks or talks) as a confirmation of their pre-existing stereotypical beliefs.

Under these adverse conditions, Terrell would be vulnerable to *stereotype threat*—as defined by people's tendency to underperform at tasks when their social group is stereotyped to be incompetent at them.[31] When Rob interrupted his presentation and implicitly called into question his technological knowledge and competence, Terrell probably became unconsciously aware of negative stereotypes about the competence and cultural fit of blacks in leading technology companies. Once activated, these stereotypes would have had a disabling impact on him. He would feel anxious. The quality of his presentation would drop. By failing to impress the senior executives at ZintZat.ai, he might have confirmed the very negative stereotypes about blacks that he had wanted to challenge. Furthermore, when no offers came his way, he would have missed out on a fleeting mainstream business opportunity.

As we contemplate the detrimental effects of pervasive negative stereotypes on minority entrepreneurs, it should be clear that the outsider problem represents a formidable challenge for them. However, the primary focus should be on uncovering code-breaking skills that can help them meet this challenge.

Notes

1. John F. Dovidio, Miles Hewstone, Peter Glick and Victoria M. Esses, "Prejudice, Stereotyping and Discrimination: Theoretical and Empirical Overview," in John F. Dovidio, Miles Hewstone, Peter Glick and Victoria M. Esses, eds., *The SAGE Handbook of Prejudice, Stereotyping and Discrimination* (London: Sage Publications Ltd., 2010), pp. 3–28; Walter Lippmann, *Public Opinion* (New York: Harcourt, Brace, 1922); Melinda Jones, *Social Psychology of Prejudice* (Saddle River, NJ: Pearson Education, 2002); David Schneider, *The Psychology of Stereotyping* (New York: Guilford Press, 2004).
2. Susan T. Fiske, Amy J. C. Cuddy, Peter Glick and Jun Xu, "A Model of (Often Mixed) Stereotype Content: Competence and Warmth Respectively Follow from Perceived Status and Competition," *Journal of Personality and Social Psychology*, vol. 82, no. 6 (2002), pp. 878–902.
3. John Oliver Siy and Sapna Cheryan, "When Compliments Fail to Flatter: American Individualism and Responses to Positive Stereotypes," *Journal of Personality and Social Psychology*, vol. 104, no. 1 (2013), pp. 87–102; John Oliver Siy and Sapna Cheryan, "Prejudice Masquerading as Praise: The Negative Echo of Positive Stereotypes," *Personality and Social Psychology Bulletin*, vol. 42, no. 7 (2016), pp. 941–954; Alexander M. Czopp, "When Is a Compliment not a Compliment? Evaluating Expressions of Positive Stereotypes," *Journal of Experimental Social Psychology*, vol. 44, no. 2 (2008), pp. 413–420; Alexander M. Czopp, Aaron C. Kay and Sapna Cheryan, "Positive Stereotypes Are Pervasive and Powerful," *Perspectives on Psychological Science*, vol. 10, no. 4 (2015), pp. 451–463; Fiske et al. (2002); Fiske et al. (2002).
4. Christopher Mims (2018).
5. Fiske et al. (2002, p. 880).
6. Anemona Hartocollis, "Harvard Rated Asian-American Applicants Lower on Personality Traits, Suit Says," *New York Times* (June 15, 2018).
7. Fiske et al. (2002).
8. Per Lundborg, "Refugees' Employment Integration in Sweden: Cultural Distance and Labor Market Performance," *Review of International Economics*, vol. 21, no. 2 (2013), pp. 219–232; Philip Oreopoulos (2011); Joan C. Williams, "The 5 Biases Pushing Women Out of STEM," *Harvard Business Review* (March 24, 2015).
9. Gordon W. Allport, *The Nature of Prejudice* (Cambridge, MA: Addison-Wesley, 1954); Gary Becker, *The Economics of Discrimination* (Chicago, London: University of Chicago Press, 1957); John F. Dovidio et al. (2010); Edward L. Glaeser, "The Political Economy of Hatred," *Quarterly Journal of Economics*, vol. 120, no. 1 (2005), pp. 45–86; Claude Steele,

Whistling Vivaldi: How Stereotypes Affect Us and What We Can Do (New York: Norton, 2010).
10. Marlene Kim, "The Working Poor: Lousy Jobs or Lazy Workers?" *Journal of Economic Issues*, vol. 32, no. 1 (1998), pp. 65–78.
11. The discussion that follows draws on these sources: Agata Antkiewicz and John Whalley, "Recent Chinese Buyout Activity and the Implications for Wider Global Investment Rules," *Canadian Public Policy/Analyse de Politiques*, vol. 33, no. 2 (2007), pp. 207–226; Peter J. Buckley, L. Jeremy Clegg, Adam R. Cross, Xin Liu, Hinrich Voss and Ping Zheng, "The Determinants of Chinese Outward Foreign Direct Investment," *Journal of International Business Studies*, vol. 38, no. 4 (2007), pp. 499–518; Yuanyuan Huang, En Xie, Yu Li and K. S. Reddy, "Does State Ownership Facilitate Outward FDI of Chinese SOEs? Institutional Development, Market Competition, and the Logic of Interdependence Between Governments and SOEs," *International Business Review*, vol. 26, no. 1 (2017), pp. 176–188; Hao Liang, Bing Ren and Sunny Li Sun, "An Anatomy of State Control in the Globalization of State-Owned Enterprises," *Journal of International Business Studies*, vol. 46, no. 2 (2015), pp. 223–240; Li-Wen Lin and Curtis J. Milhaupt, "We Are the (National) Champions: Understanding the Mechanisms of State Capitalism in China," *Stanford Law Review*, vol. 65, no. 4 (2013), pp. 697–759; Richard McGregor, *The Party: The Secret World of China's Communist Rulers* (New York: HarperCollins Publishers); David A. Ralston, Jane Terpstra-Tong, Robert H. Terpstra, Xueli Wang and Carolyn Egri, "Today's State-Owned Enterprises of China: Are They Dying Dinosaurs or Dynamic Dynamos?" *Strategic Management Journal*, vol. 27, no. 9 (2006), pp. 825–843; Huaichuan Rui and George S. Yip, "Foreign Acquisitions by Chinese Firms: A Strategic Intent Perspective," *Journal of World Business*, vol. 43, no. 2 (2008), pp. 213–226; The World Bank, *Bureaucrats in Business: The Economics and Politics of Government Ownership* (Oxford: Oxford University Press, 1995).
12. The discussion that follows draws on Gary Burnison (2011, pp. 95–107).
13. Allen et al. (2005); Meghana Ayyagari, Asli Demirgüç-Kunt and Vojislav Maksimovic, "Formal versus Informal Finance: Evidence from China," *Review of Financial Studies*, vol. 23, no. 8 (2010), pp. 3048–3097; John Bonin and Paul Wachtel, "Financial Sector Development in Transition Economies: Lessons from the First Decade," *Financial Markets, Institutions & Instruments*, vol. 12, no. 1 (2003), pp. 1–66.
14. James J. Heckman, "Detecting Discrimination," *Journal of Economic Perspectives*, vol. 12, no. 2 (1998), pp. 101–116.
15. James J. Heckman (1998); Philip Oreopoulos (2011).

16. José Mata and Claudia Alves, "The Survival of Firms Founded by Immigrants: Institutional Distance between Home and Host Country, and Experience in the Host Country," *Strategic Management Journal*, vol. 39, no. 11 (2018), pp. 2965–2991.
17. This justification is consistent with finance research which recognizes the benefits associated with long-term banking relationships, and drawbacks of centralization and credit-scoring technologies for small businesses in general, and those owned newcomers or immigrants in particular. For example, see: Allen N. Berger, Nathan H. Miller, Mitchell A. Petersen, Raghuram G. Rajan, Jeremy C. Stein, "Does Function Follow Organizational Form? Evidence from the Lending Practices of Large and Small Banks," *Journal of Financial Economics*, vol. 76, no. 2 (2005), pp. 237–269; Allen N. Berger and Gregory F. Udell, "Relationship Lending and Lines of Credit in Small Firm Finance," *Journal of Business*, vol. 68, no. 3 (1995), pp. 351–381; Allen N. Berger and Gregory F. Udell, "The Economics of Small Business Finance: The Roles of Private Equity and Debt Markets in the Financial Growth Cycle," *Journal of Banking & Finance*, vol. 22, no. 6–8 (1998), pp. 613–673; Jeremy C. Stein, "Information Production and Capital Allocation: Decentralized versus Hierarchical Firms," *Journal of Finance*, vol. 57, no. 5 (2002), pp. 1891–1921. In addition, the following study lends support to the view that comparable immigrant and native-born business owners are treated similarly when they apply for bank loans: Shaoming Cheng, "Potential Lending Discrimination? Insights from Small Business Financing and New Venture Survival," *Journal of Small Business Management*, vol. 53, no. 4, pp. 905–923. However, the bulk of the evidence points to discrimination in small business lending in the case of traditionally disadvantaged borrowers. For example, see: Elizabeth Asiedu, James A. Freeman, and Akwasi Nti-Addae, "Access to Credit by Small Businesses: How Relevant Are Race, Ethnicity and Gender?" *American Economic Review*, vol. 613, no. 1 (2012), pp. 95–107; Timothy Bates, "Minority Entrepreneurship," *Foundations and Trends in Entrepreneurship*, vol. 7, no. 3–4 (2011), pp. 151–311; David G. Blanchflower, Phillip B. Levine, and David J. Zimmerman, "Discrimination in the Small Business Credit Market," *Review of Economics and Statistics*, vol. 85, no. 4 (2003), pp. 930–943; Lloyd Blanchard, Bo Zhao and John Yinger, "Do Lenders Discriminate against Minority and Woman Entrepreneurs?" *Journal of Urban Economics*, vol. 63, no. 2 (2008), pp. 467–497; Collen Ken Casey, "Low-Wealth Minority Enterprises and Access to Financial Resources for Start-Up Activities Do Connections Matter?" *Economic Development Quarterly*, vol. 26, no. 3 (2012), pp. 252–267; Cavalluzzo and John Wolken, "Small Business Loan Turndowns, Personal Wealth and

Discrimination," *Journal of Business*, vol. 78, no. 6 (2005), pp. 2153–2178.
18. Carter et al. (2015); Stuart Fraser, "Is there Ethnic Discrimination in the UK Market for Small Business Credit?" *International Small Business Journal*, vol. 27, no. 5 (2009), pp. 583–607.
19. Fraser (2009).
20. Fraser (2009, p. 589).
21. George A. Akerlof, "The Market for 'Lemons': Quality Uncertainty and the Market Mechanism," *Quarterly Journal of Economics*, vol. 84, no. 3 (1970), pp. 488–500.
22. Dennis J. Aigner, and Glenn G. Cain, "Statistical Theories of Discrimination in Labor Markets," *Industrial and Labor Relations Review*, vol. 30, no. 1 (1977), pp. 175–187; Bradford Cornell and Ivo Welch, "Culture, Information, and Screening Discrimination," *Journal of Political Economy*, vol. 104, no. 3 (1996), pp. 542–571; Shelly J. Lundberg and Richard Starz, "Private Discrimination and Social Intervention in Competitive Labor Market," *American Economic Review*, vol. 73, no. 3 (1983), pp. 340–347.
23. Shamena Anwar, Patrick Bayer and Randi Hjalmarsson, "The Impact of Jury Race in Criminal Trials," *Quarterly Journal of Economics*, vol. 127, no. 2 (2012), pp. 1017–1055; Robert Blauner, *Race Oppression in America* (New York: Harper & Row, 1972); Eugene Genovese, *The Slaveholders' Dilemma: Freedom and Progress in Southern Conservative Thought, 1820–1860* (Columbia, SC: University of South Carolina Press, 1992); Mark Bauerlein, *Negrophobia: A Race Riot in Atlanta* (San Francisco, CA: Encounter Books, 2001); Edward L. Glaeser, "The Political Economy of Hatred," *Quarterly Journal of Economics*, vol. 120, no. 1 (2005), pp. 45–86; James McPherson, *For Cause and Comrades: Why Men Fought in the Civil War* (Oxford, UK: Oxford University Press, 1997); Claude Steele, *Whistling Vivaldi: How Stereotypes Affect Us and What We Can Do* (New York: Norton, 2010). C. Vann Woodward, *The Origins of the New South 1877–1913* (Baton Rouge, LA: Louisiana State University Press, 1951).
24. Bertrand and Mullainathan (2004).
25. Hal R. Arkes and Catherine Blumer, "The Psychology of Sunk Cost," *Organizational Behavior and Human Decision Processes*, vol. 35, no. 1 (1985), pp. 124–140; Daniel Kahneman, *Thinking Fast and Slow* (New York: Farrar, Straus & Giroux, 2011); Barry M. Staw, "The Escalation of Commitment to a Course of Action," *Academy of Management Review*, vol. 6, no. 4 (1981), pp. 577–587; Herbert A. Simon, "A Behavioral Model of Rational Choice," *Quarterly Journal of Economics*, vol. 69, no. 1 (1955), pp. 99–118; Amos Tversky and Daniel Kahneman, "Judgement

Under Uncertainty: Heuristics and Biases," *Science*, 185 (1974), pp. 1124–1130.
26. Kahneman (2011); Tversky and Kahneman (1974).
27. I apply insights from a dual process theory of how people reason, and make judgments and decisions. See the following sources: Carlos Alós-Ferrer and Fritz Strack, "From Dual Processes to Multiple Selves: Implications for Economic Behavior," *Journal of Economic Psychology*, vol. 41 (2014), pp. 1–11: Jonathan St. B. T. Evans and Keith E. Stanovich, "Dual-Process Theories of Higher Cognition: Advancing the Debate," *Perspectives on Psychological Science*, vol. 8, no. 3 (2013), pp. 223–241; Daniel Kahneman (2011).
28. Marianne Bertrand and Sendhil Mullainathan (2004); Pedro Bordalo, Katherine Coffman, Nicola Gennaioli and Andrei Shleifer, "Stereotypes," *Quarterly Journal of Economics*, vol. 131, no. 4 (2016), pp. 1753–1794; Elizabeth Gorman, "Gender Stereotypes, Same-Gender Preferences, and Organizational Variation in the Hiring of Women: Evidence from Law Firms," *American Sociological Review*, vol. 70, no. 4 (2005); pp. 702–728; Thomas E. Nelson, Michele Acker, and Manis Melvin, "Irrepressible Stereotypes," *Journal of Experimental Social Psychology*, vol. 32, no. 1 (1996), pp. 13–38; Barbara F. Reskin, The Proximate Causes of Employment Discrimination, *Contemporary Sociology*, vol. 29, no. 2 (2000), pp. 319–328; Myron Rothbart, Solomon Fulero, Christine Jensen, John Howard and Pamela Birrell, "From Individual to Group Impressions: Availability Heuristics in Stereotype Formation," *Journal of Experimental Social Psychology*, vol. 14, no. 3 (1978), pp. 237–255.
29. Vishal K. Gupta, A. Banu Goktan and Gonca Gunay, "Gender Differences in Evaluation of New Business Opportunity: A Stereotype Threat Perspective," *Journal of Business Venturing*, vol. 29, no. 2 (2014), pp. 273–288; Vishal K. Gupta, Daniel B. Turban and Ashish Pareek, "Differences Between Men and Women in Opportunity Evaluation as a Function of Gender Stereotypes and Stereotype Activation," *Entrepreneurship Theory and Practice*, vol. 37, no. 4 (2013), pp. 771–788.
30. Miles Hewstone, "The 'Ultimate Attribution Error'? A Review of the Literature on Intergroup Attributions," *European Journal of Social Psychology*, vol. 20, no. 4 (1990), pp. 311–335; Raymond S. Nickerson, "Confirmation Bias: A Ubiquitous Phenomenon in Many Guises," *Review of General Psychology*, vol. 2, no. 2 (1998), pp. 175–220; Thomas F. Pettigrew, "The Ultimate Attribution Error: Extending Allport's Cognitive Analysis of Prejudice." *Personality and Social Psychology Bulletin*, vol. 5, no. 4 (1979), pp. 461–476.
31. Carl L. von Baeyer, Debbie L. Sherk and Mark P. Zanna, "Impression Management in the Job Interview: When the Female Applicant Meets the

Male (Chauvinist) Interviewer," *Personality and Social Psychology Bulletin*, vol. 7, no. 1 (1981), pp. 45–51; Gupta et al. (2013, 2014); Margaret Shih, Todd L. Pittinsky and Nalini Ambady, "Stereotype Susceptibility: Identity Salience and Shifts in Quantitative Performance," *Psychological Science*, vol. 10, no. 1 (1999), pp. 80–83; Claude M. Steele, "A Threat in the Air: How Stereotypes Shape Intellectual Identity and Performance," *American Psychologist*, vol. 52, no. 6 (1997), pp. 613–629; Claude M. Steele and Joshua Aronson, "Stereotype Threat and the Intellectual Test Performance of African Americans," *Journal of Personality and Social Psychology*, vol. 69, no. 5 (1995), pp. 797–811.

PART II

Code-Breaking Skills

CHAPTER 5

A Growth Mindset

On July 13, 2010, there was a gathering in a convocation hall at the University of Leicester in Leicestershire, the historic county of Britain's East Midlands region. It was already past noon, and rays of sunlight were beginning to come into view as gray clouds drifted. Although the ceremony for the graduating class of 2010 was completed, many attendees remained seated for the next event: the award of an honorary (Doctor of Laws) degree. The recipient was Hilary Devey, CEO and Chairman of the Pall-Ex Group, a leading network of haulage companies in Britain.[1]

Hilary was seated on stage, next to a presenter who stood behind a podium. She held a half smile and tenderness in her eyes as the presenter read about her accomplishments, and occasionally glanced at her with a smile. After almost eight minutes into his speech, the presenter declared:

> [T]oday we honor one of the very best of our present entrepreneurs. Mr. Vice Chancellor on the recommendation of the Senate and of the Council, I present to you Hilary Devey that you may confer on her the honorary degree of Doctor of Laws.[2]

Rising to a round of applause, Hilary accepted a scrolled degree and settled behind the podium. After expressing formal greetings and gratitude for the honorary degree, she shared thoughts that offered glimpses of a journey that many present might not have known well:

I've been called many names, some flattering and some not so, one which seems to occur with increasing regularity is the word entrepreneur. People constantly ask me: "what is an entrepreneur and what are the attributes of an entrepreneur?" Well I would like to quote Machiavelli, and make of that what you will: "entrepreneurs are simply those who understand that there is little difference between obstacle and opportunity, and they are able to turn both to their own advantage."[3]

Those who knew Hilary as a teenager might not have expected her to grace the door of a university, let alone receive an honorary Degree. After all, she had already left the formal school system before turning 15 years old. However, what they might have overlooked is that she never gave up on her education. It mainly came in the form of experiential learning.

When her father's struggling heating business eventually failed, her comfortable childhood years in Bolton, North West Britain, slipped away in turbulence. In a quest for survival, moving in and out of neighborhoods had become the norm. This meant that she never had a chance to stay in one school long enough to make close friends, or daydream of what she could become. Still, she had hoped to become a veterinarian. But when she left school for good, her new found freedom would take her somewhere else.

To her father, Arthur Channon Brewster, she was just "Hils," his delightful and strong-willed daughter. Hils went to work as a teenager and never looked back. Before celebrating her sweet 16 birthday, she had already helped Arthur operate a bar and hotel. But doing so was not as fulfilling as she initially hoped. Eventually, she moved on to a receptionist job. But it was short-lived. Left stranded without a job, she turned to Arthur for advice.

"Don't ever work for anyone else," he said.[4]

But it would take several detours before Hilary heeded Arthur's advice. At one point, she sought opportunities in air traffic control after successfully taking on the grueling program of the Women's Royal Air Force (WRAF). However, as the prospects for employment weakened, she looked for opportunities elsewhere. Eventually, she landed jobs in logistics or supply chain management roles in the retail industry. Once there, she began to make her mark.

Hilary asked better questions than most people did—how can we get overnight deliveries? How do we keep trucks working with full load most of the time? How can we foster trust and cooperation among independent haulage companies? Even better, she was determined to provide better answers.

Hilary had also come to appreciate how comfortable she felt dealing with people and tough situations. She was actually very good at winning hearts and minds while selling things. These skills were already on display when she stood behind the counter of an ice-cream van as a child. Many unsuspecting parents approached the van to fetch a scoop of ice-cream for their kids, only to find themselves paying more than expected, because they just couldn't turn down the treat she offered them too.

In 1996, Hilary decided to put her haulage network ideas to the test by launching Pall-Ex. However, she needed lots of money and reputable members to make it work. One would have expected her to win over bankers, investors and haulage companies because she was contributing a lot of the required start-up capital and logistics expertise. Plus, there was a high demand for the services that her new and better haulage network would provide—retailers and others were willing to pay more for faster and better delivery services. Haulage companies should have been particularly willing to join her network because it would enable them to operate more frequently and profitably. Specifically, they could now keep their trucks working with full load because the network made it possible to trade palletized freight and delivery assignments with well-vetted partners at a centralized location.

Despite all these selling points, she struggled to make headway with her haulage network idea. At the time, she was a single mother taking care of her son, Mevlit, who was dyslexic. This certainly amplified her challenges, but she was determined to take a chance on her idea. With £60,000 in hand, she just needed £20,000 to hit her start-up funding target of £80,000. But when she pitched her business idea to a HSBC bank manager in Rayleigh, Essex, he directed her to make better use of her time and energy: "You're a woman trying to do business in a man's world and a single parent. I'm afraid that I'm not going to give you a loan. Or an overdraft."[5]

It wasn't lost on Hilary that Mevlit needed her. But whether she prioritized her business aspirations over childcare was a choice for her to make, not a banker. Ultimately, she had to sell her house, car and other personal items, such as jewelry, to raise the required capital.

But getting business from truck drivers would test her patience and will power. Like the truck driver who interrupted her membership pitch by asking: "What do you know about driving a truck, love?"[6] She could have walked away in disgust, but she held her ground and made her case for his business.

As with any new business, progress was punctuated by unexpected setbacks. But Hilary was on board for the long haul. In 2000, a new day had dawned on her when Pall-Ex crossed the million-dollar mark in profits. Nine years later, her peers in the transport industry would acknowledge and legitimize her success—she became the first woman to receive the prestigious Sir Robert Lawrence Award from the Chartered Institute of Logistics and Transport.

When the University of Leicester honored her with a Doctor of Laws degree in 2010, Hilary had also gained formal acceptance by the education system she had operated outside of, but never shunned as a lifetime learner. On that special afternoon in a convocation hall, she offered clues about her entrepreneurial success and longevity: she "[understands] that there is little difference between obstacle and opportunity, and [has been] able to turn both to [her] own advantage."[7]

* * *

On the surface, Hilary's sheer will to survive could give the impression that marginalized and minority entrepreneurs will thrive if they are smart and industrious. But the story is more complicated because intelligence and hard work alone cannot explain why some people, and not others, emerge as persistent winners in virtually every society. We've already seen that historically dominant groups can preserve their initial advantages because normal social dynamics reinforce those advantages—specifically, historically well-connected and powerful people often remain this way because they predominantly form relationships with each other, and many people want to form relationships with them.

This should remind us that deep-rooted obstacles underpin the outsider problem. At the same time, the previously shared success stories, and now Hilary's, point to code-breaking skills that can tip the balance in favor of marginalized and minority entrepreneurs. What if I told you that these virtually hidden skills embody this specific set of personal qualities and strategies: (a) growth mindset, (b) valuable knowledge from formal education, (c) strategic identity orientation, and (d) complementary social and political skills. Let's now discuss the role that a growth mindset plays, and take up the other qualities later.

To set the stage for our discussion, let's start off with the concept of opportunity because that's what all underdogs seem to lack, and keep asking for. We can think of an opportunity as a chance to do something that can create value. When the Syrian refugee Hussein Shaker first landed in Germany,[8] he desperately sought to rebuild his life by seeking out local employers. He wanted to find someone who was willing to give him an opportunity to contribute, and earn from his computer programming skills. When Hussein eventually created a satisfying job for himself by co-founding the online job portal, MigrantHire, he had recognized and exploited an opportunity that others overlooked, or even dismissed.

The core insights behind a growth mindset can help us understand why Hussein and other marginalized entrepreneurs fare better than their peers when it comes to identifying and exploiting opportunities. When people have a growth mindset, as opposed to a fixed mindset, they are more motivated to grow, and believe in their potential to do so.[9] As a result, they have an enhanced potential to achieve and sustain a high level of personal and professional development. Interestingly, the most critical aspect of this development process is not obvious because it unfolds in the brain.

Neuroscientists describe the brain as a network.[10] Specifically, it may be represented as a set of nodes and links between them. The nerve cells or neurons in the brain serve as the nodes, and stand out as specialized information receivers and transmitters. As links, synapses help create an active brain by connecting these neurons. We actually become more intelligent and better learners when more neurons are connected. This is so because greater connectivity in the brain translates into more rapid transfer of new information in the larger nervous system.

When people are motivated to grow, they are inclined to take on difficult problems. They then try to solve them by working hard, strategizing, and seeking feedback from others. Even when this approach doesn't immediately payoff in terms of material success, progress is already registered in their brains. In particular, their brains encode the new insights they gain by arranging new connections between neurons. As a result, their brains will have more neurons, and the connections between them will be stronger. In addition, their intelligence and learning potential will improve.

This kind of mental development can give marginalized and minority entrepreneurs a competitive edge. In particular, their brains can become wired in ways that help them press on in the face of disappointing news, or outright rejection. When Hilary Devey requested a £20,000 loan from a HSBC bank manager in Rayleigh, Essex, she had good reason to expect a "yes." After all, she had already committed her own money to the venture. Furthermore, she had a sound business plan, combined with substantial industry experience. Yet, the loan officer told her "no." When Jack Ma sought government support for his online directory business, China Pages, in 1995, he was told a resounding "no" in Beijing.

Anne Mulcahy, former CEO of Xerox, provides a good example of the kind of thinking that emanates from a growth mindset. "Every single no is an opportunity to reflect and ask, 'How do you get to a yes?'" she once said.[11]

Coming into view is the notion that entrepreneurs from marginalized and minority groups can achieve lasting success when they have a growth mindset. Their high potential for success reflects the continuous personal and professional development that they are likely to experience, combined with alertness to opportunities. This will become clearer when I take up the topic of entrepreneurial alertness in the next chapter.

Notes

1. This account is not meant to serve as a biography. I have tried to recreate the events, places, settings, personal characteristics and conversations based on publicly available information, including: Hilary Devey, *Bold as Brass: My Story* (London: Pan Macmillan, 2012); Popular media: Elena Moya, "Can Hilary Devey drive a truck? The Pall-Ex Founder Can Certainly Drive a Freight Revolution," *The Guardian* (October 22, 2010).
2. Primary source of quote: A YouTube clip of Hilary Devey receiving an honorary degree (Doctor of Laws) from the University of Leicester (Available online: https://www.youtube.com/watch?v=Zh5I_xFobOQ, July 13, 2010).
3. Ibid.
4. Devey (2012, p. 79).
5. Devey (2012, pp. 189–190).
6. Devey (2012, p. 191).
7. A YouTube clip of Hilary Devey receiving an honorary degree (Doctor of Laws) from the University of Leicester (Available online: https://www.youtube.com/watch?v=Zh5I_xFobOQ, July 13, 2010).
8. Meaker (2016).
9. Carol S. Dweck, *Mindset: The New Psychology of Success* (New York: Ballantine Books, 2016).

10. Olaf Sporns, *Networks of the Brain* (Cambridge, MA: The MIT Press, 2011); Larry W. Swanson, *Brain Architecture: Understanding the Basic Plan*, Second Edition (New York: Oxford University Press, 2012).
11. Gary Burnison (2011, p. 156).

CHAPTER 6

Valuable Knowledge from Formal Education

Before turning six, Mike Lazaridis was in search of a country that he could truly call his home.[1] A few years earlier, he had arrived in Turkey with his Greek parents, Nick (clothing salesman) and Dorothy (seamstress), and sister, Cleo. At the time, there was rampant intolerance toward non-Muslims. As Christians, they were on the receiving end of negative attitudes and discrimination.

But Mike's parents assured him that he could accomplish anything if he was prepared to work hard at it. This reassurance was enough to preserve his innocence while he took apart and built things around the house. Still, his parents were concerned about their safety in Turkey. So they left for Germany. After staying there for a short period, they found what turned out to be a resting place in Canada.

As newcomers to Canada, Mike and his family were relatively disadvantaged. They faced the challenge of settling, integrating and rebuilding their lives in yet another country. But fortunately for them, Canada had already begun to embrace multiculturalism as its immigrant population became more diverse around the early 1970s. So they had a chance to blossom in a generally supportive environment.

Mike started out at the W. F. Herman Secondary School in Windsor, Ontario. By grade 6, his deep love for science was already evident. He would tinker with electronics in the electrical and machine shops after classes. His electronics shop teacher, Mr. John Micsinszki, had described a future world in which amazing things would unfold as new technologies combine electronics, computers and wireless data. This captivated Mike's imaginations. But he had more questions than answers. This propelled him to visit the local public library in Windsor very often.

Having read all the science books at the library at this early stage of his life, Mike had grasped fundamental principles in math and science that might have baffled his peers. He was particularly captivated by the idea that energy is too scarce and valuable a thing to waste; and that simple things are more elegant than complex ones. These ideas would later crystalize into convictions that guided his thinking as an innovator.

His journey as an innovator was well underway by the time he enrolled in an undergraduate program in engineering and computer science at the University of Waterloo. He accelerated it by leaving university before graduation to develop, and market a digital advertising device with Douglas Fregin, a childhood friend. In 1984, they went on to co-found Research in Motion (RIM) in the small and friendly Southern Ontario city of Waterloo.

RIM's operations were housed in a three-room office above a bagel shop, nearby the technology-promoting University of Waterloo, and the business-oriented Wilfred Laurier University. It would go unnoticed by industry leaders in larger cities such as Toronto; and virtually unknown by the rest of the world.

Mike was ready to lead the hardware and software development aspects of the business. However, he needed help with the strategic positioning, financing and marketing of RIM's offerings in the marketplace. Therefore, he brought in Jim Balsillie in 1992 to take care of these functional roles. The two agreed to lead the company as co-CEOs.

Around 1995, Mike had an opportunity to take a big chance on his engineering brain. RIM had already formed a relationship with a much larger U.S.-based partner, BellSouth. It had acquired a wireless data network, Mobitex, and wanted to know whether RIM could help them capitalize on it. In particular, BellSouth wanted to increase demand for its pagers, and get ahead of large competitors, such as Motorola. At the time, pager users were reaping few benefits from their device because they were unable to instantly respond to the messages they received. As a result, there was an opportunity to add value in the marketplace by replacing one-way pagers with two-way ones.

Mike was ready to exploit this opportunity. Long guided by the principles of energy conservation and simplicity, he conceptualized small, portable and energy-efficient two-way wireless communication devices that could perform essential functions. Although the actual work turned out to be more difficult than expected, Mike and his engineering team were able to deliver the first wearable (Inter@ctive) two-way pager in 1997. However, BellSouth's customers were less than thrilled about it.

In a search for new possibilities, Mike turned his attention to wireless email. He and his team later discovered that RIM could create unique value by incorporating an email feature in an upgraded version of the two-way pager. However, before they could exploit this new opportunity, they had to quickly resolve lingering concerns about security, limited bandwidth and the lack of a wireless network under their control. They sought to address these issues by developing software that automatically redirected messages from users' email account on their desktop computers or laptops to their mobile device within a few minutes. A key step in this process was the transformation of all messages in users' email account into encrypted and compressed files. Another step was the transmission of these files over the internet to a wireless network to be sorted. Once decrypted and decompressed, users would be notified about new messages on their mobile device. They could then read and reply to them right away.

Unfortunately, BellSouth's senior executives weren't interested in this email-pager combo plan. However, they allowed RIM to pursue it as an independent initiative by providing airtime on their underutilized Mobitex network in exchange for an upfront cash payment. This would later result in the development of its basic smartphone, BlackBerry, in 1999.

In the decade that followed, RIM stunned the world with phenomenal growth and leadership. But Apple and Google took notice, and entered the game with their own smartphone platforms, iOs and Android, respectively. These platforms were supported by growing communities of independent software developers with valuable complementary offerings. As sands accumulated in its innovation engine, RIM sputtered and slipped into what seemed like unending downward spiral. Its once dominant share of the U.S. smartphone market shrunk to single digits, accompanied by deep losses, disappointed carriers and consumers, disgruntled investors, and laid off employees.

The rules of the game in the smartphone industry had rapidly and dramatically changed: consumers wanted dazzling, multifunctional smartphones with complementary applications that captured their imaginations, and satisfied their rising need for self-expression. This meant that features once dismissed as non-essential, battery-draining or bandwidth-demanding, were now in demand. Manufacturers and telecommunication service providers were now willing to help by offering more powerful batteries and more bandwidth. In this new environment, the very principles of energy conservation and simplicity were undermined.

When Mike and Jim gave up their co-CEO role in January 2012, the curtains were fully drawn on an era that once stirred dizzying excitement in Waterloo.

Now far removed from the messy business of smartphones, Mike had time to reflect on what had once brought him unadulterated delight as an innovator. I imagine that his mind went back to the simpler times of discovery and experimentation in a machine shop at W. F. Herman Secondary School. It was there where he once worked side by side with Douglas Fregin. Perhaps he recalled celebrating their winning entry in the grade 7 science fair competition; or the common aspirations that pulled them from their universities to start RIM.

Almost three decades later, they teamed up again by creating Quantum Valley Investments, a $100-million venture capital fund. On September 21, 2012, more than 5000 attendees (including the late Professor Stephen Hawking) looked forward to learn about the promise of this partnership at the grand opening of the Mike & Ophelia Lazaridis Quantum-Nano Centre, hosted by the University of Waterloo.

> "Nothing you see in the classical technology world can prepare you for what you will see in the quantum technology revolution. Doug and I have nearly 30 years' experience as inventors of the BlackBerry, creators of the smartphone industry and builders of Canada's largest global tech business … Our belief in the power of quantum physics to transform society inspired us to develop a strategy some 12 years ago that led to the world-class quantum research capability that exists in Waterloo today," said Mike.[2]

Mike's fascination with quantum technologies went all the way back to his second year at the University of Waterloo. But he's not looking to take a chance on his dream as a technology entrepreneur this time; instead, he's ready to take a chance on others by funding their promising ideas.

* * *

Like Mike, entrepreneurs that lead today's fastest-growing technology-intensive ventures often have an educational background in science, technology, engineering and mathematics (STEM) disciplines.[3] Unfortunately, proportionally few aspiring entrepreneurs from marginalized and minority groups have a strong background in these disciplines.[4] However, a substantial number of them are highly qualified, with some level of STEM-related training—including African-Americans and Hispanics in the United States,[5] immigrants in Canada,[6] BAME in the UK,[7] among others.

When Mike drove away from BlackBerry for good in 2012, quickly fading in his rear-view mirror were its glory days as a global smartphone leader. He was certainly better off than where his initial underdog status suggested he could have been. Along the way, he demonstrated an enhanced ability to identify, evaluate, develop and transform basic scientific ideas into commercially viable products and services.

These entrepreneurial processes deserve attention when contemplating what contributes to the success of initially marginalized entrepreneurs in general, and minority entrepreneurs in particular. The concept of entrepreneurial alertness deserves special attention here.[8] Research tells us that entrepreneurially alert individuals diligently and effectively perform three sets of related tasks.[9]

First, they actively scan the business environment for new events and trends; and when they find something new, they search for information about it. In today's knowledge-based global economy, they could be looking for information on any of the following trends: rise in robotics and artificial intelligence-enabled automation of business processes and operations across many industries; shift toward renewable sources of energy; shift toward ride-hailing or ride-sharing arrangements (e.g., Uber, Lyft); increasing availability of informal lodging arrangements (e.g., Airbnb); digitally enabled changes in the recruitment process (i.e., LinkedIn and Monster.com); rise in digitally enabled independent or freelance work opportunities (i.e., Uber, Etsy, Didi); development of quantum computing technologies that enable computers to rapidly perform a large number of computations at the same time; the emergence of blockchain technologies that facilitate the distributed and digital recording of transactions among parties in a customized, yet cost-effective and transparent way; and new developments in software security, cloud computing, computer vision, virtual reality, autonomous driving, drones, or 3D printing.[10]

How well entrepreneurs from marginalized and minority groups scan and search for information depends on what and who they already know.[11] We've already lamented that they start out less prepared for entrepreneurship than others because they lack relevant know-how, and have weak ties to powerful mainstream networks, if any. However, as recognized earlier, they often have a college or university education. This implies that they may have prior foundational knowledge and critical thinking skills at levels that enable them to scan and search for information in the current science- and technology-driven, global marketplace.

To be sure, they are better positioned to do so when they have valuable knowledge from formal education in business and STEM-related areas.[12] Mike started out without firsthand experience in technology commercialization. But his prior knowledge from a formal education in science and technology gave him a good start. It made him excel at scanning the science and technology space for new developments, and searching for relevant information on significant developments.

At some point, the scanning and search process will produce seemingly unrelated pieces of information on the different events and trends— including the ones we previously considered. Making sense of all of this could be a challenge. This brings us to the second set of tasks that define entrepreneurially alert entrepreneurs: they excel at associating disparate information and connecting the dots.[13]

Marginalized entrepreneurs' prior knowledge also comes into play here. Specifically, their ability to find meaning, novel insights or patterns in apparently unrelated information on various events and trends depends on what they already know.[14] For example, their prior knowledge will influence what information they highlight, downplay or dismiss. This influence could be substantial when it's unclear what to believe in the face of uncertainty or conflicting information; or when there is considerable pressure to act quickly.

After combining new information with what they already know, believe and/or expect, they might come away learning something new. This brings us to the final set of tasks that characterize entrepreneurial alertness: evaluating and judging.[15] Like every entrepreneur, those from marginalized and minority groups have to evaluate whether what they've learnt represents a novel solution to a pressing problem; or an idea about how to create new, or significantly improved, products, services, production methods, business models, or marketing and distribution methods. After doing so, they need to judge whether this solution or idea is worth exploiting in an existing organization, or a newly created venture.[16] Afterward, it's time for them to spring into action by developing an appropriate strategy to exploit the new opportunity, and mobilizing resources to execute this strategy.

Let's return to Hussein for an example of entrepreneurial alertness under very difficult circumstances.[17] His transition from an unemployed refugee in March 2015 to a co-founder of MigrantHire the same year is phenomenal because many of Germany's refugees have remained unemployed for years. But as a trained and experienced computer programmer, he didn't want his expertise to go to waste. He was motivated to grow, and contribute to the country that received him by applying his technical knowledge and skills.

Despite his initially limited knowledge of how things worked in Germany, combined with language barrier, he was alert to opportunities. Shortly after arriving in Germany, he tried to integrate by taking language classes. Around the same time, he began to diligently scan the business environment. He also searched online and offline sources for job-related information. In fact, his first call center job came from a search on eBay. But he wanted work that made better use of his expertise; therefore, he kept scanning and searching. This process culminated in a new business venture that solved a real problem: the creation of an online job portal that made it possible for job-seeking refugees and German employers to find each other quicker and cheaper.

In sum, entrepreneurs from marginalized and minority groups are likely to be entrepreneurially alert when their college or university education equips them with cutting-edge knowledge in general, and particularly in STEM-related fields. When these entrepreneurs' formal knowledge base is augmented by a growth mindset, they are especially likely to be entrepreneurially alert because they are intrinsically motivated to grow, experiment, strategize, work hard, seek feedback from others, and solve difficult problems. The solutions to some problems may very well come in the form of innovative products or services that create substantial value for new or existing companies.

Notes

1. This account is not meant to serve as a biography. I have tried to recreate the events, places, settings, personal characteristics and conversations based on publicly available information, including: Sofy Carayannopoulos, "Research in Motion: A Small Firm Commercializing a New Technology," *Entrepreneurship Theory & Practice*, vol. 29, no. 2 (2005), pp. 219–232; Claire Gagné, "Douglas Fregin—The Other RIM Guy," *Canadian Business* (December 5, 2005); Allan Levine, "Canada's Values, Then and Now," *National Post* (September 7, 2016); Jacquie McNish and Sean Silcoff, *Losing the Signal: The Spectacular Rise and Fall of BlackBerry* (Toronto: HarperCollins Publishers Ltd., 2015); "Mike Lazaridis: The

Power of Ideas," *The Science Show, ABC Radio National (Australian Broadcasting Corporation)* (June 9, 2012).
2. "Lazaridis, Fregin and $100 Million," *Exchange*, vol. 30, no. 5 (2013), p. 12.
3. Matthias Almus and Eric A. Nerlinger, "Growth of New Technology-Based Firms: Which Factors Matter?" *Small Business Economics*, vol. 13, no. 2 (1999), pp. 141–154; Robert Demir, Karl Wennberg and Alexander McKelvie, "The Strategic Management of High-Growth Firms: A Review and Theoretical Conceptualization," *Long Range Planning*, vol. 50, no. 4 (2017), pp. 431–456; Noam Wasserman, "How an Entrepreneur's Passion Can Destroy a Startup," *Wall Street Journal* (August 25, 2014).
4. Jeremy Ashkenas, Haeyoun Park and Adam Pearce, "Even with Affirmative Action, Blacks and Hispanics Are More Underrepresented at Top Colleges Than 35 Years Ago," *New York Times* (August 24, 2017); Abigail Thernstrom and Stephan Thernstrom, *No Excuses: Closing the Racial Gap in Learning* (New York: Simon & Schuster, 2003); White House Initiative on Educational Excellence for African Americans, "FACT SHEET: Spurring African-American STEM Degree Completion," U.S. Department of Education (March 16, 2016).
5. Timothy Bates, "Minority Entrepreneurship," *Foundations and Trends in Entrepreneurship*, vol. 7, no. 3–4 (2011), pp. 151–311.
6. Conference Board of Canada, *Brain Gain 2015: The State of Canada's Learning Recognition System* (Ottawa: Conference Board of Canada, 2016); Nicholas Keung, "Immigrants Are Largely Behind Canada's Status as One of the Best-Educated Countries," *The Star* (February 1, 2018).
7. Monder Ram and Trevor Jones, *Ethnic Minorities in Business* (Milton Keynes: The Small Enterprise Research Team, Open University, 2008).
8. Robert A. Baron, "Opportunity Recognition as Pattern Recognition: How Entrepreneurs 'Connect the Dots' to Identify New Business Opportunities," *Academy of Management Perspectives*, vol. 20, no. 1 (2006), pp. 104–119; Tony Fu-Lai Yu, "Entrepreneurial Alertness and Discovery," *Review of Austrian Economics*, vol. 14, no. 1, pp. 47–63; Connie Marie Gaglio, "The Role of Mental Simulations and Counterfactual Thinking in the Opportunity Identification Process," *Entrepreneurship Theory and Practice*, vol. 28, no. 6 (2004), pp. 533–552; Connie Marie Gaglio and Jerome A. Katz, "The Psychological Basis of Opportunity Identification: Entrepreneurial Alertness," *Small Business Economics*, vol. 16, no. 2 (2001), pp. 95–111; Denis A. Grégoire, Pamela S. Barr and Dean A. Shepherd, "Cognitive Processes of Opportunity Recognition: The Role of Structural Alignment," *Organization Science*, vol. 21, no. 2 (2010), pp. 413–431; Israel M. Kirzner, *Competition and Entrepreneurship* (Chicago: University of Chicago Press, 1973); Israel M. Kirzner,

"Entrepreneurial Discovery and the Competitive Market Process: An Austrian Approach," *Journal of Economic Literature*, vol. 35, no. 1 (1997), pp. 60–85; Israel M. Kirzner, "Creativity and/or Alertness: A Reconsideration of the Schumpeterian Entrepreneur," *Review of Austrian Economics*, vol. 11, no. 1–2 (1999), pp. 5–17; Israel M. Kirzner, "The Alert and Creative Entrepreneur: A Clarification," *Small Business Economics*, vol. 32, no. 2 (2009), pp. 145–152; Jeffery S. McMullen and Dean A. Shepherd, "Entrepreneurial Action and the Role of Uncertainty in the Theory of the Entrepreneur," *Academy of Management Review*, vol. 31, no. 1 (2006), pp. 132–152; Jintong Tang, K. Michele (Micki) Kacmar and Lowell Busenitz, "Entrepreneurial Alertness in the Pursuit of New Opportunities," *Journal of Business Venturing*, vol. 27, no. 1 (2012), pp. 77–94; Dave Valliere, "Entrepreneurial Alertness and Paying Attention," *Journal of Enterprising Culture*, vol. 21, no. 1 (2013), pp. 1–17.
 9. Tang et al. (2012).
10. Joe Atikian, "Robots, AI, and Jobs: All Three Are Coming," *The Globe Mail* (May 13, 2018); Davide Castelvecchi, "Quantum Computers Ready to Leap out of the Lab," *Nature*, vol. 541 (2017), pp. 9–10; Teppo Felin and Karim Lakhani, "What Problems Will You Solve with Blockchain?" MIT Sloan Management Review (September 11, 2018); Jonathan A. Knee, "Why Some Platforms Are Better Than Others," *MIT Sloan Management Review* (November 30, 2017); McKinsey Global Institute, "Technology, Jobs, and the Future of Work," McKinsey & Company (February 2017).
11. See the following related research: Alexander Ardichvili, Richard Cardozo and Sourav Ray, "A Theory of Entrepreneurial Opportunity Identification and Development," *Journal of Business Venturing*, vol. 18, no. 1 (2003), pp. 105–123; Baron (2006); Eren Ozgen and Robert A. Baron, "Social Sources of Information in Opportunity Recognition: Effects of Mentors, Industry Networks, and Professional Forums," *Journal of Business Venturing*, vol. 22, no. 2 (2007), pp. 174–192; Scott Shane, "Prior Knowledge and the Discovery of Entrepreneurial Opportunities," *Organization Science*, vol. 11, no. 4 (2000), pp. 448–469.
12. Almus and Nerlinger (1999); Bates (2011); Demir et al. (2017).
13. Tang et al. (2012).
14. Shane (2000); Tang et al. (2012).
15. Tang et al. (2012).
16. Ibid.
17. Guy Chazan, "Most Refugees to be Jobless for Years, German Minister Warns," *Financial Times* (June 22, 2017); Meaker (2106); Nicholson (2017).

CHAPTER 7

Strategic Identity Orientation

Another important item on our list of enabling qualities and strategies is a strategic identity orientation. To unpack this concept, we need to first take care of the basic concept of identity.

If the question is "Who am I?" then the answer can be found in one's self-identity.

Self-identity embodies how people define or view themselves.[1] A commonly recognized form is social identity.[2] When people have a social identity, they primarily view themselves as members of a specific social group with a distinctive set of values and beliefs. For example, some minority entrepreneurs may primarily see themselves as members of the minority community with which they are associated.

By way of illustration, consider the case of black entrepreneurs. They can proudly express a black racial identity by making the following statement: "I'm a *black* (technology) entrepreneur." As members of the black community, they are expected to embrace the same core beliefs about common challenges that black entrepreneurs face, what the solutions might be, and what opportunities are desirable. When they strongly identify with the black community, they will feel a sense of belonging and self-worth. Furthermore, they may derive substantial value from these psychosocial benefits when they live up to the ideals of the black community.

Role-based identity is another notable form of identity.[3] When people have such an identity, they primarily view themselves in terms of the roles they perform in society. For example, if some black entrepreneurs primarily have an entrepreneurial role identity, rather than a black racial identity, they would make the following statement, instead: "I'm a technology entrepreneur." When they strongly identify with an entrepreneurial role, they are likely to think and act independently of the black community.[4] This can happen because their self-worth primarily comes from living up to their own standards, or the standards or expectations of various relationship partners with whom they interact or co-create value.

In reality, entrepreneurs will not generally see themselves exclusively in terms of their group membership or entrepreneurial role. In addition to collectively interacting with, and supporting their larger communities, they have other relationships in which they carry out parental, spousal and many other roles.[5] As a result, they are contending with multiple self-identities. Therefore, we need to conceptualize how people define themselves in a more comprehensive way.

Research has addressed this issue by proposing that people's self-identity is multi-faceted, and can be described by three distinct identity orientations.[6] In line with a social identity, there is a collective identity orientation. There is also a relational identity orientation that corresponds with the previously discussed role-based identity.[7] A personal identity orientation is the third dimension of people's self-identity.[8] In this case, they primarily see themselves as individuals with personal qualities that set them apart from others. This means that they are motivated to show that they are different in ways that can create unique value. At the same time, they rank their own interests above those of their relationship partners, and the larger community with which they are associated.

This is a good place to return to the concept of a strategic identity orientation. I define it as people's tendency to enact a match between their identity orientation and external environment that advances their business interests. In other words, they have an incentive to redefine themselves as they try to navigate different social contexts because some self-conceptions serve them well in some settings, and poorly in others.

The concept of strategic identity orientation is particularly relevant in the case of entrepreneurs from marginalized and minority groups. A key point is that a single identity orientation is unlikely to serve them well in their communities and mainstream settings. Consequently, some of them will be motivated to redefine themselves in ways that enable them to effectively navigate these socially and economically different arenas.

To see why, note that a collective identity orientation is likely to serve them well in their own communities, and potentially hamper them in mainstream settings involving investors, suppliers, or customers. Let's not forget that these marginalized and minority entrepreneurs are associated with groups (i.e., immigrants, women, blacks and other racialized groups) that are often stereotyped as incompetent at certain tasks, or unfriendly in various situations.[9] Furthermore, they are particularly vulnerable to stereotype threat when they strongly identify with negatively stereotyped groups.[10]

Since a collective identity orientation can hold back marginalized and minority entrepreneurs in mainstream settings, some of them will be inclined to enact other identity orientations that serve them well in such settings. Consider the case of immigrants in Canada, a traditional destination country with over 150 years of immigration.[11] About one in five Canadians is a foreign-born person. Currently, that person is likely to originate from India, China or the Philippines, compared with earlier periods—before the Second World War and up to the 1970s—when proportionally more immigrants came from the United Kingdom, Germany and the Netherlands. Immigrants from these and other source countries are different in many ways, including their type and level of education, work experience, business experience, languages and/or dialects, wealth, motivation for migrating, and familiarity with the institutions and cultures of Canada, and where they settle.

A major challenge for immigrant entrepreneurs is how far they should go in distinguishing themselves from their co-ethnic or co-national communities in general, and particularly as they spend more time in their host countries. This is an important issue because they can draw on their communities for psychosocial (i.e., sense of belonging) and economic benefits (i.e., low-cost labor or supplies) when developing their ventures.[12] At the same time, their growth potential is limited when they primarily depend on a co-ethnic network of employees, suppliers and customers. Since some of their very employees might leave and become nearby competitors, they might struggle to operate profitably. To make things worse, they might suffer from low self-esteem when mainstream leaders perceive them as necessity entrepreneurs with low-potential business operations.

Some immigrant entrepreneurs might respond to the perceived low status of their co-ethnic communities by gravitating toward a strong collective identity orientation. They are particularly likely to do if they were pushed into entrepreneurship in the first place—possibly because they couldn't find acceptable work. Alternatively, they may take pride in contributing to business activity in their co-ethnic communities because doing so can raise these communities' profile.[13] In this case, they can realize a high self-esteem if they and their communities view such support and sacrifices as noble. They might feel an even greater sense of self-worth when leading co-ethnic members publicly acknowledge them for their selfless contributions.

On the contrary, a collective identity orientation is unlikely to appeal to immigrant entrepreneurs who want to accumulate wealth, and elevate their own social status. They are likely to turn away from their co-ethnic communities, and gravitate toward mainstream markets.[14] But going mainstream calls for some level of adaptation. One form this could take is a greater tendency toward a personal identity orientation. Such an orientation can make it easier for immigrant entrepreneurs to recognize their distinctive qualities; and attract potential mainstream players by sharing how they can add unique value in various endeavors.

Their personal identity orientation is especially likely to emerge in mainstream settings when they have valuable technical knowledge (i.e., expertise in artificial intelligence), or a high level of proficiency in the host-country official language. In this case, they may have multiple job options because leading companies are competing for their expertise. However, they may turn down attractive job offers because they are pulled into entrepreneurship. Perhaps they have already spotted a promising opportunity. They may strongly believe in their ability to convert this opportunity into a leading high-tech company. Perhaps they need to mobilize additional resources. If so, perhaps they want a chance to show private equity investors what they are good at, and how their venture will create value. In this case, their personal identity orientation is likely to serve them better than a collective identity orientation.

It is important to recognize that entrepreneurship itself can be a catalyst for a personal identity orientation in immigrant entrepreneurs. Compared with salaried employment, it provides more opportunities for them to express their differences in ways that reveal their distinctiveness, and the unique value they can create.[15] In other words, entrepreneurship can normalize a personal identity orientation. Beyond gravitating toward a socially accepted identity orientation, immigrant entrepreneurs will derive a psychological advantage when they enact a personal identity orientation. Specifically, they will be less vulnerable to stereotype threat than their peers who embrace a collective identity; and hence, better positioned to deliver great results as entrepreneurs.[16]

Interestingly, immigrant entrepreneurs may enjoy a similar psychological advantage in mainstream settings when they exhibit a relational identity orientation. Such an orientation can come about if they perceive themselves primarily as relationship partners. Specifically, they could see themselves as part of a larger innovation ecosystem, inhabited by investors, suppliers, customers, and other potential partners. In this context, they want to form productive and mutually beneficial partnerships, and add value by performing an entrepreneurial role very well. The more strongly they identify with this role and the potential value they can co-create with others, the less vulnerable they might be to stereotype threat. As a result, they will be in a good position to interact effectively with mainstream partners and co-create value.

As much as entrepreneurs from marginalized and minority groups can get ahead when they embrace a personal or relational identity orientation, these identity orientations cannot fully meet their psychological needs. In particular, they could miss out on valuable psychosocial benefits (i.e., a sense of belonging) associated with a collective identity orientation, or strong identification with their communities. Besides, even if they do not desire such benefits, they may still want to contribute to their communities by giving back in one way or another. Their mental and physical health could suffer if they feel unfulfilled in these areas.[17]

This situation points to trade-offs between personal or relational identity orientation and collective identity orientation. In other words, entrepreneurs from marginalized and minority groups need to appropriately switch between identity orientations as they move between different social contexts to keep their need for distinctiveness and a sense of belonging in balance.[18] In short, they need to have a strategic identity orientation. This kind of identity orientation necessarily requires marginalized and minority entrepreneurs to adopt a reasonably dynamic, or flexible, view of themselves.[19]

For an example of how this might work, come along with me to two places where the former US President Barack Obama once visited. Turning my eyes to Capitol Hill, I can see him delivering the State of the Union address in 2015:

> We are 15 years into this new century. Fifteen years that dawned with terror touching our shores; that unfolded with a new generation fighting two long and costly wars; that saw a vicious recession spread across our nation and the world. It has been, and still is, a hard time for many. But tonight, we turn

the page … Will we accept an economy where only a few of us do spectacularly well? Or will we commit ourselves to an economy that generates rising incomes and chances for everyone who makes the effort… So the verdict is clear. Middle-class economics works. Expanding opportunity works. And these policies will continue to work, as long as politics don't get in the way.[20]

Looking back six years earlier, I can also see the former US president pulling up in Chicago at a chili-dog restaurant in a predominantly black neighborhood. He's about to enjoy a delicious hot dog when the cashier asked whether he needed any change. To the delight of the cashier, his response confirmed he was leaving a tip: "Naw, we straight!"[21]

In these two scenes, code switching is on display. As you can see, it's essentially a linguistic strategy. When executed well, this strategy can help marginalized and minority entrepreneurs effectively navigate different circles of contacts by appropriately switching between languages, dialects and/or accents. A strategic identity orientation calls for this kind of flexibility and much more.[22]

Since switching between different identity orientations can be challenging and mentally burdensome,[23] marginalized and minority entrepreneurs who view themselves more flexibly than their peers perhaps differ from them in important ways. In particular, they might differ in terms of how they perceive themselves, others, tasks, and the business environment. In addition, they are likely to share several things in common with mainstream business leaders, including knowledge, experiences, and languages or dialects.

Many marginalized enterprising individuals have gained the cross-cultural knowledge required for inter-cultural engagement long before they sought to launch their career or business. When Indra Nooyi arrived in the United States from Chennai, she didn't settle in an ethnic enclave dominated by Indian co-nationals; instead, she was immersed in a distant mainstream culture at Yale University. As a boy, Jack Ma had routinely interacted with foreigners at a local hotel in Hangzhou. He tried to learn English, and later traveled to Australia in his twenties. Meanwhile, Clarence Wooten moved between Baltimore's black-dominated inner cities and white-dominated suburbs during his formative years. As a result, he became exposed to computers and the internet long before his African-American peers.

In short, a strategic identity orientation is a critical success factor for entrepreneurs from marginalized and minority groups.

Notes

1. Viktor Gecas, "The Self-Concept," *Annual Review of Sociology*, vol. 8, no. 1 (1982), pp. 1–33; Sheldon Stryker and Peter J. Burke, "The Past, Present, and Future of an Identity Theory," *Social Psychology Quarterly*, vol. 63, no. 4 (2000), pp. 284–297.
2. George A. Akerlof and Rachel E. Kranton, "Economics and Identity," *Quarterly Journal of Economics*, vol. 115, no. 3 (2000), pp. 715–753; Michael A. Hogg and Deborah J. Terry, "Social Identity and Self-Categorization Processes in Organizational Contexts," *Academy of Management Review*, vol. 25, no. 1 (2000), pp. 121–140; Michael A. Hogg, Deborah J. Terry, Katherine M. White, "A Tale of Two Theories: A Critical Comparison of Identity Theory with Social Identity Theory," *Social Psychology Quarterly*, vol. 58, no. 4 (1995), pp. 255–269; Russell Spears, "The Interaction between the Individual and the Collective Self: Self-Categorization in Context," in Constantine Sedikides and Marilynn B. Brewer, eds., *Individual Self, Relational Self, Collective Self* (Philadelphia, PA: Psychology Press, 2001), pp. 171–198; Jan E. Stets and Peter J. Burke, "Identity Theory and Social Identity Theory," *Social Psychology Quarterly*, vol. 63, no. 3 (2000), pp. 224–237; Henri Tajfel, "Social Identity and Intergroup Behavior," *Social Science Information*, vol. 13, no. 2 (1974), pp. 65–93; Henri Tajfel, *Social Identity and Intergroup Relations* (Cambridge: Cambridge University Press, 1982); Peggy A. Thoits and Lauren K. Virshup, "Me's and We's: Forms and Functions of Social Identities," in Richard D. Ashmore and Lee Jussim, eds., *Self and Identity: Fundamental Issues* (New York: Oxford University Press, 1997), pp. 133–158; John C. Turner, "Social Comparison and Social Identity: Some Prospects for Intergroup Behaviour," *European Journal of Social Psychology*, vol. 5, no. 1 (1975), pp. 5–34.
3. Hogg et al. (1995); Spears (2001); Stets and Burke (2000); Thoits and Virshup (1997).
4. Stets and Burke (2000).
5. Stets and Burke (2000); Thoits and Virshup (1997).
6. For a more comprehensive treatment of the multi-faceted nature of identity, see the following studies: Marilynn B. Brewer and Wendi Gardner, "Who Is This 'We'? Levels of Collective Identity and Self Representations," *Journal of Personality and Social Psychology*, vol. 71, no. 1 (1996), pp. 83–93; Shelley Brickson, "The Impact of Identity Orientation on Individual and Organizational Outcomes in Demographically Diverse Settings," *Academy of Management Review*, vol. 25, no. 1 (2000), pp. 82–101.
7. Ibid.

8. Ibid.
9. Fiske et al. (2000).
10. Shih et al. (1999); Steele (2010); Valerie Purdie-Vaughns, Claude M. Steele, Paul G. Davies, Ruth Ditlmann and Jennifer Randall Crosby, "Social Identity Contingencies: How Diversity Cues Signal Threat or Safety for African Americans in Mainstream Institutions," *Journal of Personality and Social Psychology*, vol. 94, no. 4 (2008), pp. 615–630.
11. Ninette Kelley and Michael J. Trebilcock, *The Making of the Mosaic: A History of Canadian Immigration Policy*, Second Edition (Toronto: University of Toronto Press, 2010); Statistics Canada, "150 Years of Immigration in Canada," Government of Canada, June 29, 2016. Available Online: https://www150.statcan.gc.ca/n1/pub/11-630-x/11-630-x2016006-eng.htm (Accessed June 20, 2018).
12. Howard E. Aldrich and Roger Waldinger, "Ethnicity and Entrepreneurship," *Annual Review of Sociology*, vol. 16 (1990), pp. 111–135; Arturs Kalnins and Wilbur Chung, "Social Capital, Geography, and Survival: Gujarati Immigrant Entrepreneurs in the U.S. Lodging Industry," *Management Science*, vol. 52, no. 2 (2006), pp. 233–247; Jennifer Lee, "Retail Niche Domination Among African American, Jewish, and Korean Entrepreneurs: Competition, Coethnic Advantage and Disadvantage," *American Behavioral Scientist*, vol. 42, no. 9 (1999), pp. 1398–1416; Ivan Light and Stavros Karageorgis "The Ethnic Economy," in Neil Smelser and Richard Swedberg, eds., *The Handbook of Economic Sociology* (Princeton, NJ: Princeton University Press, 1994), pp. 647–669; Alejandro Portes and Robert L. Bach, *Latin Journey: Cuban and Mexican Immigrants in the United States* (Berkeley, CA: University of California Press, 1985); Alejandro Portes, Robert D. Manning, "The Immigrant Enclave: Theory and Empirical Examples," in Susan Olzak and Joane Nagel, eds., *Comparative Ethnic Relations* (Orlando, FL: Academic Press, 1986), pp. 47–68; Min Zhou, "Revisiting Ethnic Entrepreneurship: Convergencies, Controversies, and Conceptual Advancements," *International Migration Review*, vol. 38, no. 3 (2004), pp. 1040–1074.
13. Hermann Achidi Ndofor and Richard L. Priem, "Immigrant Entrepreneurs, the Ethnic Enclave Strategy, and Venture Performance," *Journal of Management*, vol. 37, no. 3 (2011), pp. 790–818.
14. Rajeswararao (Raj) S. Chaganti, Allison D. Watts, Radha Chaganti and Monica Zimmerman-Treichel, "Ethnic-Immigrants in Founding Teams: Effects on Prospector Strategy and Performance in New Internet Ventures," *Journal of Business Venturing*, vol. 23, no. 1 (2008), pp. 113–139; Ndofor and Priem (2011).
15. Dean A. Shepherd and Holger Patzelt, *Entrepreneurial Cognition: Exploring the Mindset of Entrepreneurs* (Cham, Switzerland: Palgrave Macmillan, 2018).

16. Naomi Ellemers, Russell Spears and Bertjan Doosje, "Self and Social Identity," *Annual Review of Psychology*, vol. 53 (2002), pp. 161–186.
17. The lack of adequate psychosocial benefits may hurt marginalized and minority entrepreneurs by amplifying the personal problems that entrepreneurs generally face. For a deeper understanding of this issue, see the following studies: E. Holly Buttner, "Entrepreneurial Stress: Is It Hazardous to Your Health?" *Journal of Managerial Issues*, vol. 4, no. 2 (1992), pp. 223–240; Muhammad Jamal, "Job Stress, Type-A Behavior, and Well-Being: A Cross-Cultural Examination," *International Journal of Stress Management*, vol. 6, no. 1 (1999), pp. 57–67; Hatun Ufuk and Özlen Özgen, "Interaction between the Business and Family Lives of Women Entrepreneurs in Turkey," *Journal of Business Ethics*, vol. 31, no. 2 (2001), pp. 95–106.
18. Blake E. Ashforth, Glen E. Kreiner and Mel Fugate, "All in a Day's Work: Boundaries and Micro Role Transitions," *Academy of Management Review*, vol. 25, no. 3 (2000), pp. 472–491.
19. Shepherd and Patzelt (2018) suggest that the overall well-being of entrepreneurs could depend on how well they keep the need for distinctiveness and a sense of belonging in balance. See the following source for a related account: Dean A. Shepherd and J. Michael Haynie, "Birds of a Feather Don't Always Flock Together: Identity Management in Entrepreneurship," *Journal of Business Venturing*, vol. 24, no. 4 (2009), pp. 316–337.
20. AFP, "Key Quotes from Obama's State of the Union Address," *Daily Nation* (January 21, 2015).
21. R.L.G., "Code-Switching: How Black to Be?" *The Economist* (April 10, 2013).
22. More generally, I articulate a view of a flexible identity that builds on, and extends the idea of code switching. The latter is primarily focused on how people navigate their own cultures and mainstream ones by switching between languages, dialects and/or accents—for example, see: Anna De Fina, "Code-Switching and the Construction of Ethnic Identity in a Community of Practice," *Language in Society*, vol. 36, no. 3 (2007), pp. 371–392; Judith N. Martin and Thomas K. Nakayama, *International Communication in Contexts*, Fifth Edition (New York: The McGraw-Hills Companies Inc., 2010); Zadie Smith, "Speaking in Tongues," *The New York Review of Books* (February 28, 2009); Vershawn Ashanti Young, Rusty Barrett, Y'Shanda Young-Rivera and Kim Brian Lovejoy, *Other People's English: Code-Meshing, Code-Switching, and African-American Literacy* (New York: Teachers College Press, 2014). As can be seen from my conceptualization of a flexible identity, it goes well beyond the adoption of a linguistic strategy for navigating different cultures.
23. Ashforth et al. (2000).

CHAPTER 8

Complementary Social and Political Skills

It's difficult for entrepreneurs from marginalized and minority groups to get ahead without interacting with dominant mainstream players. Even if they have a commercially viable idea for an innovative product or service, they're unlikely to convert this idea into a thriving business in the current global marketplace with just relatives and friends. At the same time, they will find it challenging to attract and work with mainstream business partners that have the funds, expertise and contacts they desperately need.

This situation is a reflection of the relatively weak position from which marginalized and minority entrepreneurs pursue critical players in mainstream markets, including workers, private equity investors, banks, suppliers, customers, and competitors. They approach such players relatively disadvantaged by virtue of their outsider status, and the negative stereotypes that others consciously or unconsciously hold about them. Therefore, sometimes the most they expect is merely a chance to show that they can do something that offers unique value.

But dominant mainstream partners, like business angels or venture capital funds, are skeptical. Sometimes they like minority entrepreneurs' business ideas, but are doubtful about their ability to execute it. Other times they have misgivings about both their ability and ideas. Clarence is familiar with skeptical mainstream investors. While operating his cash-strapped ImageCafe venture in Baltimore, he had desperately sought funding from private equity investors. On one occasion, he ran into William R. Daniels on a flight to San Francisco. William was a well-connected stockbroker in the angel investor community at the time.[1]

Within a few seconds of their exchange, Clarence left a positive impression on William, so much so that he later shared: "If sheer force of will ensures success, he [Clarence] will be successful."[2] William and his co-investors went on to offer Clarence $116,000 in exchange for an ownership stake of 11.6 percent in ImageCafe. However, William later admitted that he had initially found it difficult to convince his skeptical and predominantly white co-investors to take a chance on Clarence and his promising internet venture. "It's not like he went to Stanford Business School. How many Internet businesses come out of Baltimore? Not a whole lot," said William.[3]

Although Clarence was grateful for the chance to take his venture to the next level, he was disappointed. "I've seen guys go in with nothing more than an idea and walk out with $1 million," he once said.[4] He wondered whether he was given less funds than his white peers primarily because of his race. As other minority entrepreneurs try to mobilize resources to grow their ventures, they will also pursue mainstream business partners; and consequently, might also end up in business relationships that they may find unsatisfying, stressful and conflict-prone.

More generally, they face the specific challenge of initiating and managing business relationships in mainstream markets to their advantage. Their ability to meet this challenge could come down to how well they create and sustain positive first impressions in their encounters with key players in the corporate world.[5] Ultimately, they have to persuade various influential groups of people outside their inner circle of relatives and friends to take actions that advance their ventures—from busy investors with more lucrative investment options, talented workers with more prestigious and financially rewarding job offers, suppliers with more creditworthy clients to picky customers preoccupied with shiny offers elsewhere.[6] And just when they think their work is done, they have to deal with government authorities to make sure they comply with laws and regulations, or benefit from certain support programs.

This brings us to the final set of code-breaking skills: social and political skills. Let's start with social skills.

We can think of socially skilled people as those with an enhanced ability to do things like[7]: (a) reading and understanding others in terms of their traits, intentions and motives, (b) presenting themselves in ways that leave a lasting positive impression on others, (c) expressing their emotions—

that is, instant and intense sensations—and feelings—that is, long-term response to emotions—in ways that bring out enthusiasm in others,[8] (d) getting people to agree with them or change their views or behaviors, and (e) fitting in a wide range of social settings. In short, these capabilities imply that socially skilled people are socially perceptive, good at impression management, expressive, and socially adaptive.

Turning to political skills, we can think of politically skilled people as individuals with an enhanced ability to do things like[9]: (a) reading and understanding others in terms of their traits, intentions and motives, (b) interacting with people who generally don't question the motives behind their actions toward them or others, (c) fitting in a wide range of social settings in ways that enable them to achieve their goals, and (d) winning and sustaining support from a group of people by getting them to agree with them, or change their views or behaviors. In sum, these capabilities suggest that politically skilled people are socially perceptive, apparently sincere, socially adaptive and influential, and good at negotiating with others in the networks they build and sustain, respectively.

On the surface, social and political skills seem to be almost identical: both set of skills capture people's ability to effectively interact with others in a wide range of social settings, and understand how they think and what they want. However, political skills go beyond social skills by specifically capturing people's ability to carefully probe for helpful or advantageous information or cues while interacting with others in various situations.[10] Politically skilled people are particularly keen to learn important things about others, and actively monitor how others perceive them. When they realize people don't perceive them as they want to be seen, they're motivated and able to change their perceptions by deploying an appropriate impression-management tactic. That is, the tactic that is most effective when trying to get others to think, feel and act in ways that advance their personal or business interests in a given situation.[11]

For example, if they learn that influential contacts are skeptical about their business acumen, they may engage in self-promotion tactics by speaking about their skills, qualifications, or accomplishments in ways that enhance their credibility. Meanwhile, they will deploy ingratiation tactics, such as flattery, in an apparently sincere way when they judge that these contacts perceive them as unfriendly or unhelpful.

What I have in mind here and elsewhere is honest impression management, not deceptive impression management or faking.[12] People who engage in this kind of dishonest behavior are likely to fail at getting others to view them favorably because it can irreparably damage their credibility. Furthermore, they may suffer from negative feelings due to the perceived lack of authenticity—stemming from the disconnect between how they really see themselves and how they want others to see them. Therefore, I specifically expect socially and politically skilled people to honestly and appropriately highlight the desirable attributes (i.e., verifiable skills, qualifications, or accomplishments) that they actually have when they engage in self-promotion; and speak sincerely, favorably and appropriately about the qualities they actually admire in others, and their organizations when they engage in ingratiation tactics.

Hilary had long honed her social and political skills while selling ice-cream on the street, and working in a pub environment during her formative years.[13] She was good at connecting with diverse people, figuring out what made them tick, and then using this information to tactically pursue her own interests—without, of course, making others worse off.

Her social and political skills were instrumental in the very survival of Pall-Ex in the early years. For instance, less than a year after starting the company's hub operations in the village of Wymesmold, half-way between the cities of Nottingham and Leicester, Pall-Ex almost came to an abrupt end with an eviction notice from the local council. While still actively recruiting new members, Hilary tried to buy time by pleading her case to the councilors. They reluctantly gave her a few months to leave the site. But that was just enough time she needed to find a new location and save her business.

In line with this example, research shows that new ventures are relatively financially successful—as reflected in high rates of sales growth, profitability, job creation or survival—when they are led by entrepreneurs who are socially and politically skilled.[14] This is largely attributed to their enhanced ability to perform various tasks that support business development, including: selling their ideas, offerings and themselves; selecting suitable employees, suppliers or business partners; negotiating; attracting private equity investors (i.e., business angels and venture capital funds), talented workers or new customers; and building, sustaining and leveraging a large network of diverse contacts.[15]

Socially and politically skilled entrepreneurs from marginalized and minority groups are likely to similarly perform these tasks relatively well, and give their ventures a competitive edge. Furthermore, even before they decide to start a business, their social and political skills might have already set them up for success by helping them get hired and promoted in leading companies.[16] If so, they probably came to their ventures with more relevant know-how and management skills than their peers. Since social and political skills are helpful for building and sustaining large networks with diverse contacts,[17] perhaps they also already established ties with key mainstream players, such as investors. This would have put them in a strong position to develop and grow their ventures because they may later turn to such players for advice, funding, endorsements, or referrals on favorable terms.[18]

Returning to the theme on first impressions, I particularly expect socially and politically skilled entrepreneurs from marginalized and minority groups to effectively use impression management tactics to deal with common obstacles linked to negative stereotypes or the lack of legitimacy.[19]

When Aisha Addo,[20] a Toronto-based community advocate and entrepreneur, launched the ride-sharing startup DriveHer in 2018, she was acting on an opportunity to solve problems that women in the ride-sharing industry have long encountered: as passengers, they need more transportation options that guarantee a safe space at all times; and as drivers, they need others to perceive and treat them as legitimate players in a male-dominated, ride-sharing industry.

As a black female technology entrepreneur in this industry, I imagine that Aisha is aware of these issues. After all, she had previously founded Power to Girls Foundation, a non-profit organization that sought to empower marginalized young girls. Before all of this, she was a business student at George Brown College, set to graduate in 2013. At the time, she hadn't yet contemplated being an entrepreneur as a career path. However, she evolved into one as she sought to advance women's social and economic welfare in the face of lingering negative stereotypes and other barriers.

Research suggests that marginalized and minority entrepreneurs can overcome these obstacles if they can get key mainstream players to perceive them as reasonably confident, competent and credible.[21] They may do so by projecting an image that embodies these qualities during the very first moment of their first interaction with such partners.[22] Unfortunately, they have very little time to do so because it can take as little as 100 milliseconds, or in the blink of an eye,[23] for an influential business partner to form an opinion about them.

This implies that marginalized and minority entrepreneurs will generally find it difficult to land a positive first impression when it matters most. And even when they do so, they have to work hard to sustain it. To do so, they have to establish an extraordinary track record; and appropriately adjust their projected image in response to relevant new insights from self-reflection, feedback from others, or changes in the external environment.[24] In practice, they need to ensure that others consistently perceive them in favorable ways during both face-to-face and online interactions. This means that they have to be selective about what they share (i.e., advice, beliefs, accomplishments, or acknowledgements) or seek (i.e., information, advice, funding, or contacts) during various face-to-face meetings; as well as social media (i.e., LinkedIn, Twitter, YouTube, Facebook, Instagram, or blogs) engagements[25]—including profile descriptions, status updates, posted articles, pictures or videos; how they present themselves and content using such channels; and what organizations, events or causes they are associated with.

Every time they leave lasting positive first impressions on others, they are actually creating and reinforcing a reputation, or personal brand, that credibly promises others something that they value.[26] This could mean that those with whom they interact are primed to act favorably toward them the very first moment they see their names. This kind of potent personal branding can help immigrant, refugee, black, Asian, Hispanic, women and other marginalized entrepreneurs transcend the narrow boxes that others put them in. It can do so by neutralizing negative stereotypes that others consciously or unconsciously hold about the capabilities of their groups (i.e., blacks and Hispanics).[27]

To conceptualize how this neutralization process could play out, imagine that some high-status, or powerful, mainstream players have just glanced at the names of some prominent ethnic minority entrepreneurs. Cognitive psychology research suggests that these players will be inclined to access non-stereotypical thoughts that can suppress, or override, the fast, unconscious and bias-prone mental processes ("system 1") that drive stereotypical beliefs and discriminatory actions.[28] When this happens, these players may also self-regulate by censoring such beliefs and actions.[29]

As a result, slow, conscious, and unbiased mental processes ("system 2") are likely to prevail and govern their thinking and judgments. In particular, these mental processes may redirect their attention to salient pieces of information or cues about well-branded ethnic minority entrepreneurs that strongly convey their reasonable confidence, competence and credibility. In other cases where these entrepreneurs' associated groups (e.g., Asians) are stereotyped as cold,[30] a personal branding strategy that effectively projects their interpersonal and team-playing skills could make others perceive them as likeable too. The same kind of mental processes can work in their favor by neutralizing negative stereotypes about their sociability.

All of this means that socially and politically skilled entrepreneurs from marginalized and minority groups are less likely to be exposed to prejudicial or discriminatory actions than their peers. This is possible because entrepreneurs can seduce even risk-conscious and disciplined mainstream players, such as private equity investors (e.g., business angels or venture capitalists), into making investment offers when they apply impression management tactics. Specifically, entrepreneurs who receive funding from these investors often do well at deploying impression management tactics (i.e., self-promotion, ingratiation and exemplification) that make others perceive them as reasonably confident, competent, credible and likeable innovators.[31] They are also likely to gain support from mainstream customers and various stakeholders when they similarly project a positive image of themselves and their fledging ventures.[32]

What should be clear is that social and political skills in general, impression management strategies in particular, will help marginalized and minority entrepreneurs develop and grow their new ventures or existing companies. At this point, a fully loaded toolkit of code-breaking skills is now within their reach. What is needed is a coherent conceptual framework that connects the dots, and uncovers critical insights. Let's take up this task in the next chapter.

NOTES

1. The Staff of the Wall Street Journal, *Breakaway: Small Business: An e-book Anthology* (New York: Simon & Schuster, Inc., 2001).
2. Ibid, p. 157.
3. Ibid.
4. Ibid, p. 158.
5. The importance of first impressions in interpersonal interactions is reflected in previous social psychology studies, including the following seminal studies: S. E. Asch, "Forming Impressions of Personality," *Journal of Abnormal Psychology*, vol. 41, no. 2 (1946), pp. 258–290; Susan T. Fiske and Steven L. Neuberg, "A Continuum of Impression Formation, from Category-Based to Individuating Processes: Influences of Information and Motivation on Attention and Interpretation," *Advances in Experimental Social Psychology*, vol. 23 (1990), pp. 1–74; Ted L. Huston and George Levinger,

"Interpersonal Attraction and Relationships," *Annual Review of Psychology*, vol. 29 (1978), pp. 115–156; William H. Turnley and Mark C. Bolino "Achieving Desired Images While Avoiding Undesired Images: Exploring the Role of Self-Monitoring in Impression Management," *Journal of Applied Psychology*, vol. 86, no. 2 (2001), pp. 351–360; Janine Willis and Alexander Todorov, "First Impressions: Making up Your Mind after a 100-Ms Exposure to a Face," *Psychological Science*, vol. 17, no. 7 (2006), pp. 592–598.
6. Young Rok Choi and Dean A. Shepherd, "Stakeholder Perceptions of Age and Other Dimensions of Newness," *Journal of Management*, vol. 31, no. 4 (2005), pp. 573–596; Matthew Rutherford and Paul Buller, "Searching for the Legitimacy Threshold," *Journal of Management Inquiry*, vol. 16, no. 1 (2005), pp. 78–92.
7. Robert A. Baron and Candida G. Brush, "The Role of Social Skills In Entrepreneurs' Success: Evidence from Videotapes of Entrepreneurs' Presentations," in P. D. Reynolds, W. D. Bygrave, N. M. Carter, S. Manigart, C. M. Mason, G. D. Meyer and K. G. Shaver, eds., Frontiers of Entrepreneurship (Wellesley, MA: Babson College, 1999), pp. 79–91; Robert A. Baron and Jintong Tang, "Entrepreneurs' Social Skills and New Venture Performance: Mediating Mechanisms and Cultural Generality," *Journal of Management*, vol. 35, no. 2 (2009), pp. 282–306; David J. Deming, "The Growing Importance of Social Skills in the Labor Market," *Quarterly Journal of Economics*, vol. 132, no. 4 (2017), pp. 1593–1640.
8. Emotions constitute the instant and intense sensations—for example, anger, fear, joy or sadness—people temporarily experience in response to specific situations or events. For example, a worker could become angry when she learns that her teammate complained to their supervisor about the quality of her work. Feelings represent people's long-term response to emotions and related circumstances (e.g., bitterness, contentment or worry). Returning to our example: after thinking about the many times she had covered for her teammate, she now feels bitter toward her co-worker. See the following sources: Panteleimon Ekkekakis, "Affect, Mood, and Emotion," in Gershon Tenenbaum, Robert C. Eklund and Akihito Kamata, eds., *Measurement in Sport and Exercise Psychology* (Champaign, IL: Human Kinetics, 2012), pp. 321–332; James A. Russell and Lisa Feldman Barrett, "Core Affect, Prototypical Emotional Episodes, and Other Things Called Emotion: Dissecting the Elephant," *Journal of Personality and Social Psychology*, vol. 76, no. 5 (1999), pp. 805–819.
9. Samuel B. Bacharach, *Get Them on Your Side: Win Support, Convert Skeptics, Get Results* (La Crosse, WI: Platinum Press, 2005); Kathleen K. Ahearn, Gerald R. Ferris, Wayne A. Hochwarter, Ceasar Douglas and

Anthony P. Ammeter, "Leader Political Skill and Team Performance," *Journal of Management*, vol. 30, no. 3 (2004), pp. 309–327; Gerald R. Ferris, Darren C. Treadway, Robert W. Kolodinsky, Wayne A. Hochwarter, Charles J. Kacmar, Ceasar Douglas and Dwight D. Frink, "Development and Validation of the Political Skill Inventory," *Journal of Management*, vol. 31, no. 1 (2005), pp. 126–152; Pamela L. Perrewé, Gerald R. Ferris, Dwight D. Frink and William P. Anthony, "Political Skill: An Antidote for Workplace Stressors," *Academy of Management Perspectives*, vol. 14, no. 3 (2000), pp. 115–123.
10. Ahearn et al. (2004); Ferris et al. (2005).
11. Kenneth J. Harris, K. Michele Kacmar, Suzanne Zivnuska and Jason D. Shaw, "The Impact of Political Skill on Impression Management Effectiveness," *Journal of Applied Psychology*, vol. 92, no. 1 (2007), pp. 278–285.
12. I recognize the distinction between honest versus deceptive impression management, and the preference for the former, as captured in the following previous studies: Joshua S. Bourdage, Nicolas Roulin and Julia Levashina, "Editorial: Impression Management and Faking in Job Interviews," *Frontiers in Psychology*, vol. 8 (2017), pp. 1–4; Anne Jansen, Cornelius J. König, Eveline H. Stadelmann and Martin Kleinmann, "Applicants' Self-Presentational Behavior: What Do Recruiters Expect and What Do They Get?" *Journal of Personnel Psychology*, vol. 11 (2012), pp. 77–85; Julia Levashina and Michael A. Campion, "Measuring Faking in the Employment Interview: Development and Validation of an Interview faking Behavior Scale," *Journal of Applied Psychology*, vol. 92, no. 6 (2007), pp. 1638–1656.
13. Devey (2012).
14. Baron and Tang (2009).
15. Baron and Tang (2009); Ruolian Fang, Lei Chi, Manli Chen and Robert A. Baron, "Bringing Political Skill into Social Networks: Findings from a Field Study of Entrepreneurs," *Journal of Management Studies*, vol. 52, no. 2 (2015), pp. 175–212; Thomas Lans, Vincent Blok and Judith Gulikers, "Show Me Your Network and I'll Tell You Who You Are: Social Competence and Social Capital of Early-Stage Entrepreneurs," *Entrepreneurship & Regional Development*, vol. 27, no. 7–8 (2015), pp. 458–473; Neil Tocher, Sharon L. Oswald, Christopher L. Shook and Garry Adams, "Entrepreneur Political Skill and New Venture Performance: Extending the Social Competence Perspective," *Entrepreneurship & Regional Development*, vol. 24, no. 5–6 (2012), pp. 283–305.
16. I draw on insights from the following studies: Maura A. Belliveau, Charles A. O'Reilly III and James B. Wade, "Social Capital at the Top: Effects of Social Similarity and Status on CEO Compensation," *Academy of*

Management Journal, vol. 39, no. 6 (1995), pp. 1568–1593; David J. Deming, "The Growing Importance of Social Skills in the Labor Market," *Quarterly Journal of Economics*, vol. 132, no. 4 (2017), pp. 1593–1640; Wayne A. Hochwarter, L. A. Witt, Darren C. Treadway and Gerald R. Ferris, "The Interaction of Social Skill and Organizational Support on Job Performance," *Journal of Applied Psychology*, vol. 91, no. 2 (2006), pp. 482–489; Ferris et al. (2005); Anne Smith, Donde Plowman, Dennis Duchon and Amber M. Quinn, "A Qualitative Study of High-Reputation Middle Managers: Political Skills and Successful Outcomes," *Journal of Operations Management*, vol. 27, no. 6 (2009), pp. 428–443.

17. Robert A. Baron and Gideon D. Markman, "Beyond Social Capital: How Social Skills Can Enhance Entrepreneurs' Success," *Academy of Management Executive*, vol. 14, no. 1 (2000), pp. 106–116; Gerald R. Ferris, Darren C. Treadway, Pamela L. Perrewé, Robyn L. Brouer, Ceasar Douglas, Sean Lux, "Political Skill in Organizations," *Journal of Management*, vol. 33, no. 3 (2007), pp. 290–320; Li-Qun Wei, Flora F. T. Chiang and Long-Zeng Wu, "Developing and Utilizing Network Resources: Roles of Political Skill," *Journal of Management Studies*, vol. 49, no. 2 (2012), pp. 381–402.

18. Fang et al. (2015); Lans et al. (2015).

19. The importance of legitimacy for business development is emphasized in previous studies, including the following: Toby E. Stuart, Ha Hoang and Ralph C. Hybels, "Interorganizational Endorsements and the Performance of Entrepreneurial Ventures," *Administrative Science Quarterly*, vol. 44, no. 2 (1999), pp. 315–349; Sze-Sze Wong and Wai Fong Boh, "Leveraging the Ties of Others to Build a Reputation for Trustworthiness among Peers," *Academy of Management Journal*, vol. 53, no. 1 (2010), pp. 129–148; Monica A. Zimmerman and Gerald J. Zeitz, "Beyond Survival: Achieving New Venture Growth by Building Legitimacy," *Academy of Management Review*, vol. 27, no. 3 (2002), pp. 414–431.

20. CBC News, *Women-Only Ride-Sharing Service DriveHer Launches Friday in Toronto* (March 15, 2018). Available online: https://www.cbc.ca/news/canada/toronto/driveher-launch-1.4578541 (Accessed November 25, 2018); StartUp Here Toronto, *GBC Entrepreneur Spotlight: Aisha Addo* (October 5, 2018). Available online: https://startupheretoronto.com/partners/startgbc/gbc-entrepreneur-spotlight-aisha-addo/ (Accessed November 26, 2018).

21. These desirable qualities are consistent with those reported in the following study: David A. Thomas and John J. Gabarro, *Breaking Through: The Making of Minority Executives in Corporate America* (Boston: Harvard Business Review Press, 1999).

22. Asch (1946); Fiske and Neuberg (1990); Huston and Levinger (1978); Willis and Todorov (2006).
23. This observation is consistent with previous social psychology research, such as Willis and Todorov (2006). In addition, scientists have found that human eyes can identify an image flashed before them for 13–80 milliseconds. See the following source for more details: Mary C. Potter, Brad Wyble, Carl Erick Hagmann and Emily S. McCourt, "Detecting Meaning in RSVP at 13 ms per Picture," *Attention, Perception, & Psychophysics*, vol. 76, no. 2 (2014), pp. 270–279.
24. Manel Khedher, "A Brand for Everyone: Guidelines for Personal Brand," *Journal of Global Business Issues*, vol. 9, no. 1 (2015), pp. 19–27; Francine Schlosser, Deborah M. McPhee and Janice Forsyth, "Chance Events and Executive Career Rebranding: Implications for Career Coaches and Nonprofit HRM," *Human Resource Management*, vol. 56, no. 4 (2017), pp. 571–591.
25. Colleen Connolly-Ahern and S. Camille Broadway, "The Importance of Appearing Competent: An Analysis of Corporate Impression Management Strategies on the World Wide Web," *Public Relations Review*, vol. 33, no. 3 (2007), pp. 343–345; Robert Lee and Oswald Jones, "Networks, Communication and Learning during Business Start-up: The Creation of Cognitive Social Capital," *International Small Business Journal*, vol. 26, no. 5 (2008), pp. 559–594; Claudia Smith, J. Brock Smith and Eleanor Shaw, "Embracing Digital Networks: Entrepreneurs' Social Capital Online," *Journal of Business Venturing*, vol. 32, no. 1 (2017), pp. 18–34.
26. For the discussion in this section, I draw on the following sources: Dennis A. Gioia, Aimee L. Hamilton and Shubha D. Patvardhan, "Image Is Everything: Reflections on the Dominance of Image in Modern Organizational Life," *Research in Organizational Behavior*, vol. 34 (2014), pp. 129–154; Erving Goffman, *The Presentation of Self in Everyday Life* (New York: Doubleday Anchor Books, 1959); Robin M. Kowalski and Mark R. Leary, "Strategic Self-Presentation and the Avoidance of Aversive Events: Antecedents and Consequences of Self-Enhancement and Self-Depreciation," *Journal of Experimental Social Psychology*, vol. 26, no. 4 (1990), pp. 322–336; Daniel J. Lair, Katie Sullivan and George Cheney, "Marketization and the Recasting of the Professional Self: The Rhetoric and Ethics of Personal Branding," *Management Communication Quarterly*, vol. 18, no. 3 (2005), pp. 307–343; Lauren I. Labrecque, Ereni Markos and George R. Milne, "Online Personal Branding: Processes, Challenges, and Implications," *Journal of Interactive Marketing*, vol. 25, no. 1 (2011), pp. 37–50; Rebecca Pera, GiampaoloViglia and Roberto Furlan, "Who Am I? How Compelling Self-storytelling Builds Digital Personal Reputation," *Journal of Interactive Marketing*, vol. 35 (2016), pp. 44–55;

Tom Peters, "The Brand Called You," *Fast Company*, no. 10 (1997), 83–90; Iris Vilnai-Yavetz and Sigal Tifferet, "A Picture Is Worth a Thousand Words: Segmenting Consumers by Facebook Profile Images," *Journal of Interactive Marketing*, vol. 32 (2015), pp. 53–69.
27. Fiske et al. (2002); Laura Morgan Roberts, "Changing Faces: Professional Image Construction in Diverse Organizational Settings," *Academy of Management Review*, vol. 30, no. 4 (2005), pp. 685–711.
28. See Bordalo et al. (2016); Patricia G. Devine, "Stereotypes and Prejudice: Their Automatic and Controlled Components," *Journal of Personality and Social Psychology*, vol. 56, no. 1 (1989), pp. 5–18; Evans and Stanovich (2013); Kahneman (2011); Nelson et al. (1996); Reskin (2000).
29. See Walter Mischel, Aaron L. DeSmet and Ethan Kross, "Self-Regulation in the Service of Conflict Resolution," in Peter T. Coleman, Morton Deutsch and Eric C. Marcus, eds., *The Handbook of Conflict Resolution: Theory and Practice*, Third Edition (San Francisco: Jossey-Bass, 2014), pp. 310–330; Mark Muraven and Roy F. Baumeister, "Self-Regulation and Depletion of Limited Resources: Does Self-control Resemble a Muscle? *Psychological Bulletin*, vol. 126, no. 2 (2000), pp. 247–259.
30. Fiske et al. (2002).
31. Cécile Carpentier and Jean-Marc Suret, "Angel Group Members' Decision Process and Rejection Criteria: A Longitudinal Analysis," *Journal of Business Venturing*, vol. 30, no. 6 (2015), pp. 808–821; Steven N. Kaplan, Berk A. Sensoy and Per Strömberg, "Should Investors Bet on the Jockey or the Horse? Evidence from the Evolution of Firms from Early Business Plans to Public Companies," *Journal of Finance*, vol. 64, no. 1 (2009), pp. 75–115; Andrew L. Maxwell and Moren Lévesque, "Trustworthiness: A Critical Ingredient for Entrepreneurs Seeking Investors," *Entrepreneurship Theory and Practice*, vol. 38, no. 5 (2014), pp. 1057–1080; Annaleena Parhankangas and Michael Ehrlich, "How Entrepreneurs Seduce Business Angels: An Impression Management Approach," *Journal of Business Venturing*, vol. 29, no. 4 (2014), pp. 543–564.
32. Greg Fisher, Donald F. Kuratko, James M. Bloodgood and Jeffrey S. Hornsby, "Legitimate to Whom? The Challenge of Audience Diversity and New Venture Legitimacy," *Journal of Business Venturing*, vol. 32, no. 1 (2017), pp. 52–71; Michael Lounsbury and Mary Ann Glynn, "Cultural Entrepreneurship: Stories, Legitimacy, and the Acquisition of Resources," *Strategic Management Journal*, vol. 22, no. 6–7 (2001), pp. 545–564; Brian G. Nagy, Jeffrey M. Pollack, Matthew W. Rutherford and Franz T. Lohrke, "The Influence of Entrepreneurs' Credentials and Impression Management Behaviors on Perceptions of New Venture Legitimacy," *Entrepreneurship Theory and Practice*, vol. 36, no. 5 (2012), pp. 941–965.

PART III

Putting It All Together and Drawing Lessons

CHAPTER 9

An Integrative Framework

We need to avoid taking either of two extreme positions when contemplating solutions to the outsider problem: that the system is too rigged for individual effort to make a difference; or that it is entirely up to individuals to make the most of a tough and unfair world.

We're a product of everything that happens to us through external forces, and the personal decisions or choices that we make at critical points in our lives.[1] Therefore, a balanced approach to the outsider problem calls for an integrative framework that clarifies the nature of the contest between personal factors and external forces.

I answer this call by conceptualizing such a framework. Buried in the rich details of the theoretical insights, evidence and moving stories I've recounted is the following basic insight: while the outsider problem holds back all underdog entrepreneurs, their personal qualities and strategies can help them succeed against the odds. What we have is a duel-like contest between the outsider problem in one corner, and their personal qualities and strategies in another corner. If the latter prevail, they win; otherwise, they're on the losing end. To better understand how this contest plays out, let's turn to the conceptual framework shown in Fig. 9.1.

This framework tells us that marginalized and minority entrepreneurs will experience a higher level of learning, capability development and financial success when the outsider problem is less severe (i.e., associated negative impact is small), and/or when they have an adequate mix of enabling

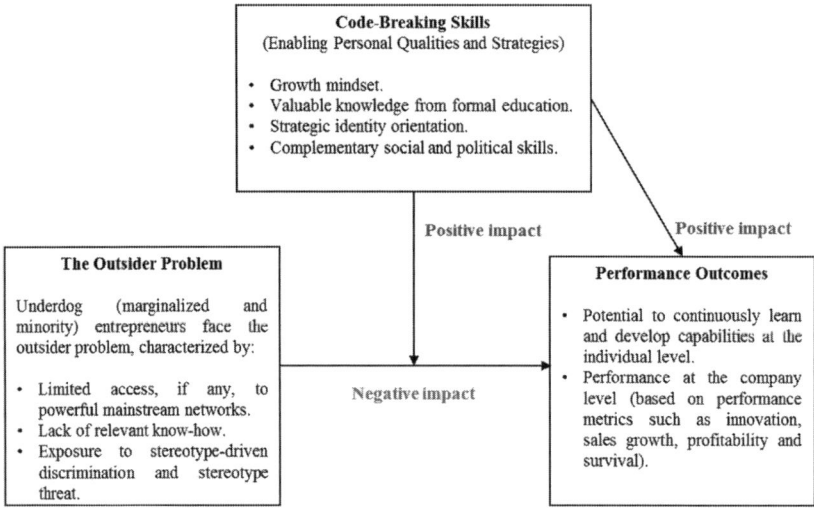

Fig. 9.1 Marginalized and minority entrepreneurs who develop the requisite code-breaking skills can overcome the outsider problem and thrive

personal qualities and strategies (i.e., associated direct and indirect positive effects are large).

We've already seen that the outsider problem embodies formidable external barriers—that is, lack of access to critical networks, lack of relevant know-how, stereotype-driven discrimination and stereotype threat. These barriers impede marginalized and minority entrepreneurs by making it difficult for them to identify, evaluate, develop and exploit opportunities. Alternatively, even if they recognize and favorably evaluate opportunities, they need to formulate an appropriate strategy to exploit them. However, they often struggle to mobilize the resources required to execute this strategy. This in turn undermines the potential of their companies to innovate, profitably grow and survive.

But there is more to the story. Some marginalized and minority entrepreneurs have personal qualities and strategies that translate into sustained superior learning and capability development at the individual level; and sustained superior performance at the company level. As previously discussed, these enabling characteristics embody a growth mindset, valuable knowledge from formal education, strategic identity orientation, and complementary social and political skills. They help marginalized entrepreneurs succeed by directly enhancing their ability to keep learning and developing their capabilities. They also indirectly help by neutralizing, or tempering, the adverse consequences of the outsider problem for their personal and business development.

As I will show in the remaining chapters, this integrative framework offers several lessons that entrepreneurs from diverse marginalized and minority groups (i.e., immigrants, racialized groups, women, among others) will find helpful.[2] Importantly, the differences between these groups do not necessarily mean that they have fundamentally different problems or issues. Instead, those differences could mean that some aspects of the outsider problem are more relevant, or more acute, for some groups than others. As a result, some marginalized and minority entrepreneurs will benefit more than others when they cultivate certain personal qualities and strategies.

For example, the outsider problem is particularly acute for black entrepreneurs looking to start science- or technology-intensive ventures in today's global knowledge-based economy. In particular, they are virtually absent from leading innovation ecosystems in the United States, Canada, Britain and elsewhere. In addition, they are hampered by negative stereotypes that call their ability to lead such ventures into question. This means that they are especially exposed to intended or unintended discrimination and stereotype threat. To make things worse, they are likely to come to these ventures less prepared than others because they have had fewer opportunities to gain substantial experience as senior executives in leading global corporations. For all these reasons, the future prospects of black entrepreneurs with science- or technology-based ventures significantly depends on how well they cultivate and deploy all the code-breaking skills we have considered.

More generally, it is appropriate to view the framework as a customizable or flexible conceptual tool that can be used to analyze and address the outsider problem in a wide range of cases. On the one hand, it facilitates a general assessment and response to the common challenges that many marginalized and minority entrepreneurs face. On the other hand, it supports a targeted response to specific issues that a particular group of entrepreneurs face. And of course, individual entrepreneurs can draw on this framework when trying to get to the next level in their entrepreneurial journey. Taken together, this framework sets up all marginalized and minority entrepreneurs for lasting success.

Notes

1. By recognizing the interplay between external and personal factors in observed performance differences between individuals or groups, I follow others who depart from the less balanced view that personal or situational factors exclusively shape people. For example, see: psychology researchers such as Douglas T. Kenrick and David Funder, "Profiting from Controversy: Lessons from the Person-Situation Debate," *American Psychologist*, vol. 43, no. 1 (1988), pp. 23–34; economics researchers such as Lawrence A. Boland, "Towards a Useful Methodology Discipline," *Journal of Economic Methodology*, vol. 8, no. 1 (2001), pp. 3–10; and economic sociology researchers such as Mark Granovetter, "Economic Action and Social Structure: The Problem of Embeddedness," *American Journal of Sociology*, vol. 91, no. 3 (1985), pp. 481–510.
2. The proposed framework (i.e., Fig. 9.1.) also adds to previous entrepreneurship research on the potential for adverse circumstances to create conditions or experiences that make disadvantaged people fit for entrepreneurship by fostering certain enabling personal qualities (i.e., work discipline, tolerance for risk, perseverance and creativity). A notable example of this line of research is the following: Danny Miller and Isabelle Le Breton-Miller, "Underdog Entrepreneurs: A Model of Challenge-Based Entrepreneurship," *Entrepreneurship Theory and Practice*, vol. 41, no. 1 (2017), pp. 7–17. I specifically add to this research stream by proposing fundamental psychosocial drivers of personal development and business success among marginalized and minority entrepreneurs, including a growth mindset and strategic identity orientation. Going one step further, I also contribute by explaining how enabling personal qualities and strategies is related to the proposed outsider problem, and ultimately, performance at the individual and firm levels.

CHAPTER 10

Commit to Ongoing Learning and Capability Development

There are several lessons that entrepreneurs from marginalized and minority groups can draw from this book. A critical one is that they can achieve and sustain success if they keep learning and developing their capabilities. To see why, think of entrepreneurship as a potentially costly experiment.[1] This experiment can produce amazing results when enterprising individuals are motivated to learn how to perform various entrepreneurial tasks better. But they need to first understand how entrepreneurial learning works.

If they are actually learning, one would expect them to accumulate novel and valuable knowledge at critical points in their entrepreneurial journey.[2] When this occurs, they will change their beliefs or perceptions about themselves, others, tasks, existing problems and solutions, how to create and deliver unique value, and/or the business environment on a whole.[3] Consequently, they will also change their strategies or behaviors in ways that lead to progress. In particular, they will progressively recognize and exploit more attractive opportunities. This can happen because progress could mean becoming more capable.[4] It could also mean doing a better job at formulating and executing strategies that can deliver faster growth, higher profitability; and ultimately, a higher chance of survival.[5]

This kind of active and performance-enhancing learning is at work in marginalized and minority entrepreneurs when they are alert to opportunities.[6] It is initiated every time they scan the business environment, and search for relevant information on a new development. It unfolds as they try to discover new actionable insights by combining what they've found with what they already know. The mental and behavioral aspects of learning are manifested when they come up with a new promising idea that leads to new, or significantly improved, products, services, processes, or organizational forms.

However, as impressive as these forms of innovation can be, they will fail to generate value in the marketplace if these entrepreneurs are not learning as well as they should. Perhaps they have the courage to take a chance on a business idea. That's great! But rushing to create a new venture to offer an untested new product or service could be a mistake. Let's not forget that 50 percent or more new businesses will involuntarily close down before getting to the five-year mark in many industries.[7] Therefore, a key benefit of entrepreneurial learning is an enhanced ability to conserve limited resources by failing quickly and cheaply.[8]

Marginalized and minority entrepreneurs should especially embrace this view because they can't afford to chase marginal or money-losing opportunities with their limited resources. Starting with their idea for a new or improved product or service, they can avoid wasting time and money by actively learning what their target customers really value. But sometimes these customers don't clearly understand their underlying problems; and even when they do, they may not conceive the most helpful or valuable solutions. Therefore, the most innovative entrepreneurs will initially formulate a logical and testable view (or theory) of specific problems, and novel solutions that can solve them. This is something they could do on their own, or preferably, within a small team of co-founders and advisers with complementary expertise. However, since innovation is about coming up with novel solutions that create unique value, they need feedback from customers before finalizing any product concept. When they solicit such feedback, they will learn which potential features their target customers count as value-added ones, and hence, which features to prioritize in an upgraded version of their product concept. They can try to further refine it through subsequent rounds of interaction with their target customers and others. When carried out well, this iterative learning process may converge on the least costly, novel offering that is validated in the marketplace.[9]

This learning process does not stop here. In a dynamic and competitive global marketplace, they have to anticipate and appropriately respond to changes. For example, their customers' tastes can change; or existing or new competitors may introduce new and improved products in the marketplace. These were exactly the kind of changes that brought down Mike and his BlackBerry team. Leading up to their fall, they had received a lot of feedback from smartphone users that called into question the suitability of their capabilities for hardware development, as opposed to secure software applications. In other words, they should have pivoted away from hardware to software applications. Eventually they did, but almost too late.[10]

If enterprising individuals from marginalized and minority groups want to get better outcomes as entrepreneurs, they need to be keen on these learning-related issues. They will need to do even more if they are primarily motivated to start a business because they cannot find acceptable work (i.e., immigrants or refugees), or viable pathways to top management in the corporate world (i.e., blacks, Hispanics, Asians or women). As necessity entrepreneurs, they start out with considerably more learning to do in a shorter time than others. This is so because they come to their ventures less prepared than others in many ways.

In particular, they've had limited opportunities to accumulate valuable knowledge through prior learning-by-doing on the job, or interpersonal learning in leading networks. This implies they need to learn at a relatively fast pace over the course of developing and growing their ventures. At the same time, they need time to reflect and draw meaningful lessons along the way. Therefore, trying to learn too quickly could mean learning less.

What is needed is a comprehensive plan that can help them learn more before they start a business, and learn at a reasonable pace afterward. This plan calls for a combination of strategies aimed at bolstering initial learning-by-doing on the job, and ongoing interpersonal learning in partnerships or networks. Let's primarily focus on the former now, and discuss the latter in greater detail later.

We already know that many minority entrepreneurs come to their ventures with a useful knowledge base from college or university education.[11] This is certainly a point in their entrepreneurial journey where they can set themselves up for success later. They can specifically do so by capitalizing on opportunities to participate in work-study or internship programs at companies ranging from startups to multinational corporations.

When appropriately designed, internship programs can enhance their entrepreneurial learning potential in a number of ways. In particular, these programs can help them move beyond textbook concepts and facts by identifying, assimilating and applying practical knowledge on various business functions and processes—that is, idea commercialization, marketing and sales, or supply chain management.[12] In addition, they will have opportunities to hone their problem-solving skills, and develop a deeper understanding of the business environment.[13] Since these programs often lead to follow-on permanent job opportunities,[14] they can also help aspiring minority entrepreneurs deepen and broaden their practical knowledge base through on-the-job, learning-by-doing. Another benefit is an opportunity to join organizational networks and learn from experts.

One cannot take it for granted that marginalized and minority entrepreneurs will have a passion for ongoing learning and capability development. But they are very likely to have it when they also have a growth mindset. Therefore, this is a personal quality that they especially need to cultivate.

Notes

1. William R. Kerr, Ramana Nanda and Matthew Rhodes-Kropf, "Entrepreneurship as Experimentation," *Journal of Economic Perspectives*, vol. 28, no. 3 (2014), pp. 25–48.
2. Teppo Felin and Todd R. Zenger, "Entrepreneurs as Theorists: On the Origins of Collective Beliefs and Novel Strategies," *Strategic Entrepreneurship Journal*, vol. 3, no. 2 (2009), pp. 127–146; J. Michael Haynie, Dean Shepherd, Elaine Mosakowski and Christopher Earley, "A situated metacognitive model of the entrepreneurial mindset," *Journal of Business Venturing*, vol. 25, no. 2 (2010), pp. 217–229.
3. Brian T McCann and Govert Vroom, "Opportunity Evaluation and Changing Beliefs During the Nascent Entrepreneurial Process," *International Small Business Journal*, vol. 33, no. 6 (2015), pp. 612–637.
4. Christopher Pryor, Justin W. Webb, R. Duane Ireland David J. Ketchen, Jr., "Toward an Integration of the Behavioral and Cognitive Influences on the Entrepreneurship Process," *Strategic Entrepreneurship Journal*, vol. 10, no. 1 (2016), pp. 21–42.
5. Ibid.
6. Tang et al. (2012).
7. U.S. Bureau of Labor Statistics, Entrepreneurship and the U.S. Economy. Retrieved from https://www.bls.gov/bdm/entrepreneurship/bdm_chart3.htm (Chart 3. Survival rates of establishments, by year started and number of years since starting, 1994–2015, in percent) (Accessed December 12, 2018); John Watson and Jim Everett, "Small Business Failure Rates: Choice of Definition and Industry Effects," *International Small Business Journal*, vol. 17, no. 2 (1999), pp. 31–47.
8. Eric Ries, *The Lean Startup: How Today's Entrepreneurs Use Continuous Innovation to Create Radically Successful Businesses* (New York: Crown Business, 2011).

9. Ries' (2011) lean start-up approach provides entrepreneurs with general guidance on this proposed iterative learning process. However, I offer a nuanced perspective that is consistent with the following recent study: Teppo Felin, Alfonso Gambardella, Scott Stern, and Todd Zenger, "Lean Startup and the Business Model: Experimentation Revisited," *Long Range Planning* (In Press, Corrected Proof). Available online at: https://doi.org/10.1016/j.lrp.2019.06.002. In this study, a key concern is that the lean start-up approach can lead to incremental, low-value innovation (as opposed to radical, high-value innovation) in new ventures because it promotes early and excessive reliance on customer feedback. I address this concern by specifically calling on entrepreneurs to initially formulate a testable theory of customer problems and potential novel solutions.
10. Shane Dingman, "BlackBerry's Focus on Software Starting to Pay Off: CEO," *The Globe and Mail* (December 18, 2015).
11. Bates (2011); Conference Board of Canada (2016); Keung (2018); Ram and Jones (2008).
12. Sue Campbell Clark, "Enhancing the Educational Value of Business Internships," *Journal of Management Education*, vol. 27, no. 4 (2003), pp. 472–484; Sarah Cooper, Colin Bottomley and Jillian Gordon, "Stepping Out of the Classroom and up the Ladder of Learning: An Experiential Learning Approach to Entrepreneurship Education," *Industry and Higher Education*, vol. 18, no. 1 (2004), pp. 11–22; David A. Kolb, Richard E. Boyatzis and Charalampos Mainemelis, "Experiential Learning Theory: Previous Research and New Directions," in Robert J. Sternberg, Li-fang Zhang, eds., *Perspectives on Thinking, Learning, and Cognitive Styles* (Mahwah, NJ: Lawrence Erlbaum, 2001), pp. 227–247; Patricia R. McCarthy and Henry M. McCarthy, "When Case Studies Are Not Enough: Integrating Experiential Learning into Business Curricula," *Journal of Education for Business*, vol. 81, no. 4 (2006), pp. 201–204; Taylor, M. Susan, "Effects of College Internships on Individual Participants," *Journal of Applied Psychology*, vol. 73, no. 3 (1988), pp. 393–401.
13. Ibid.
14. Jack Gault, Evan Leach and Marc Duey, "Effects of Business Internships on Job Marketability: The Employers' Perspective," *Education & Training*, vol. 52, no. 1 (2010), pp. 76–88.

CHAPTER 11

Strategically Cultivate Mutually Beneficial Networks

Entrepreneurs from marginalized and minority groups need to effectively cultivate mutually beneficial networks that span their communities and mainstream markets because their very survival depends on them.

We have already seen that high-status or powerful networks in mainstream society play a critical role in all phases of the entrepreneurial process, from recognizing opportunities to exploiting them. They are a key source of advantage for new ventures because they can provide exclusive access to resources—including experience-based know-how, funding on favorable terms, and legitimacy—that are valuable, unique, and difficult or costly to imitate.[1] Furthermore, they foster ongoing learning and capability development.[2]

With so much at stake, disadvantaged minority entrepreneurs have to rethink how they respond to being on the outside of leading mainstream networks. A common response is to retreat from such networks by creating their own cohesive and homogenous communities or associations. These minority-only networks are desirable because they offer psychosocial benefits and relief from negative stereotypes. However, they are less helpful for learning and innovation than large networks with diverse connections.

We already know that the essence of innovation is the novel recombination of existing knowledge in ways that create value in the marketplace.[3] More recombination possibilities imply greater potential for innovation. To come up with many recombination possibilities, we need a diverse knowledge base to begin with. This kind of knowledge base is the outcome of a purposeful search for information from diverse sources, or contacts with diverse backgrounds. Alternatively, it comes from intentionally cultivating large and diverse networks.

The potential for such networks to foster superior innovation performance is evident in the case of Mike and his BlackBerry team. Their ability to drive smartphone innovation was constrained by the exhaustible or redundant imagination, knowledge and skills of a small and cohesive organizational network of software developers. They would later drop out of the smartphone innovation race as their rivals (i.e., Apple and Google) introduced more novel innovations, powered by an ever-growing open network of independent, diverse software developers.

In this digital age, it is possible for entrepreneurs to strategically develop, manage and benefit from large and diverse networks of online (i.e., LinkedIn, Facebook, Twitter and other social media platforms) and offline relationships. These relationships can range from acquaintances, or weak ties (i.e., friends of one's friends), to people whom they know very well and trust, or strong ties (i.e., relatives and close friends or long-time business associates).[4] While weak ties are more helpful when seeking novel information, strong ties are more willing to provide experience-based know-how and other complementary benefits (i.e., funding on favorable terms and endorsement).[5]

If minority entrepreneurs are motivated to grow their networks, they can do so by developing weak ties in a variety of ways. Starting with their pre-existing strong ties, they can broaden their networks by asking these strong ties to introduce them to their contacts.[6] This can be done electronically (i.e., via email), or in person. Alternatively, they can directly initiate new relationships online by sending an invitation or friendship request to the friends of their friends on social media platforms, such as LinkedIn or Facebook.[7] If they have a Twitter account, they can also form weak ties by simply following well-connected individuals with expertise in their areas of interest.[8] And of course, attending relevant industry events outside their communities is another way to develop weak ties.

They have to be purposeful and strategic when growing their networks. Since networking can be time consuming, they should commit to daily, weekly or monthly networking activity at levels that allow them to stay productive as entrepreneurs. In particular, they need to ensure that they have sufficient time to develop an innovative and validated product or service, build a founding or top management team, fine-tune their sales and marketing plan, raise funds, acquire new customers, or streamline their operations. More generally, they need time to reflect, learn and come up with new ideas that can sustain their innovation performance.

They should pursue mutually beneficial networks by actively managing them. A major concern is that larger and more diverse networks may merely help minority entrepreneurs come within reach of novel information, experience-based know-how and other complementary network benefits. To actually maximize their chance of both reaching and acquiring such benefits, they need to achieve and maintain an optimal mix of weak and strong ties.[9]

Over time, they need to recognize that some acquaintances and close friends will become more critical than others for the next stage of their entrepreneurial journey—possibly because of what they know, who they know, or the kind of psychosocial support they provide. On the contrary, some strong ties can transform into counterproductive or even detrimental relationships.[10] They have to anticipate and appropriately deal with these situations. Specifically, while staying close to productive strong ties, they should proactively convert critical weak ties into strong ones. Their social and political skills will come into play because they need to develop relationships that are built on mutual attraction, mutual trust and reciprocity (i.e., helping each other solve task-related problems).[11]

They are already off to a good start if they are motivated to show potential partners what they can do for them, rather than merely expect to get help from them. Building on this outlook, they need to figure out the norms, or unwritten rules, that govern social interaction and exchange in their specific situation, whether online or offline. The previous emphasis on impression also applies here: they have to ensure that potential mainstream contacts have an initially positive view of them. And of course, they need to sustain this positive first impression. In addition to using appropriate impression management tactics, they need to be thoughtful when making requests. In particular, they need to know what requests (i.e., funding, endorsement, advice or referral) are appropriate, when is the right time to ask someone for a favor, where and how best to do so.

The general picture is that minority entrepreneurs have to be prepared to engage in frequent, intimate and mutually satisfying face-to-face interactions to convert acquaintances into allies. In other words, they have to relationally embed them in their networks. However, doing so will leave them with less available time, money and energy to stay connected to the many acquaintances that enrich their networks. Fortunately, research shows that they can maintain satisfactory relationships with a large pool of weak ties by structurally embedding them.[12] The key goal here is to get as many of their acquaintances to know each other as possible. Entrepreneurs can significantly increase the number of mutual acquaintances in their networks when they join social media networks (i.e., LinkedIn and Twitter), professional bodies or industry associations, within and outside their communities.

However, their ability to fully benefit from structurally embedded ties online will depend on their contributions, and the overall quality of their interactions with others in such virtual settings.[13] They need to actively engage with others in meaningful and helpful ways. In the case of LinkedIn, they can do so in several ways. For example, they may like the posts of others, endorse their skills, provide helpful feedback on posted questions or issues, share news about events of interest to others, or support a charitable event. Importantly, too, they need to figure out, and conform to the norms that govern social interaction and exchange on their specific social media platform.

In online communities such as LinkedIn and Twitter, they need to be aware that their contacts or followers are likely to frown on the use of overt self-promotion or marketing tactics—for example, claiming to the best entrepreneur, claiming to have the best products or services, or prematurely making unsolicited sales pitches.[14] In addition, an online community might want to know their members on a personal level before they fully embrace the business-related content they share. In some cases, it is sufficient to share a lesson learnt from a failed exam, or lost deal, that can help others avoid the same mistake. It's perhaps a bad idea to share intimate or mundane details about their daily lives—like what they've had for breakfast, lunch and dinner.[15]

Although online networks are becoming more important for business development,[16] they lack the instant and helpful nonverbal cues (i.e., facial expressions) that accompany face-to-face interactions.[17] Therefore, minority entrepreneurs need to be very thoughtful when interacting with others online to avoid serious misunderstandings, or costly mistakes. In addition, based on impression management considerations, they need to be selective about who they follow or endorse, and what content they post or share (i.e., articles, comments, pictures, or videos). They also need to evaluate and appropriately deploy social media platforms' capabilities or features—that is, digital user profile, search, relation management and network transparency features—in ways that optimize their potential to contribute to, and benefit from, their online communities.[18]

In the case of LinkedIn, potential contacts are likely to find and gravitate toward minority entrepreneurs when they have publicly available, error-free user profiles that warmly and credibly signal their business acumen, and the quality of their ventures. LinkedIn contacts are also inclined to initiate a relationship with them when they have many mutual friends, followers or connections. Minority entrepreneurs can make new friends on LinkedIn by following a similar pattern of profile review and connection initiation.

By acting on these insights and advice, marginalized and minority entrepreneurs can overcome, or at least reduce, network-related barriers that block their pathways to learning, innovation and success.

Notes

1. Aldrich and Fiol (1994); Jay Barney, "Firm Resources and Sustained Competitive Advantage," *Journal of Management*, vol. 17, no. 1 (1991), pp. 99–120; Gedajlovic et al. (2013); Zimmerman and Zeitz (2002).
2. Johanson and Vahlne (2009).
3. D. Charles Galunic and Kathleen M. Eisenhardt, "Architectural Innovation and Modular Corporate Forms," *Academy of Management Journal*, vol. 44, no. 6 (2001), pp. 1229–1249; Samina Karim and Aseem Kaul, "Structural Recombination and Innovation: Unlocking Intraorganizational Knowledge Synergy through Structural Change," *Organization Science*, vol. 26, no. 2 (2014), pp. 439–455; Joseph A. Schumpeter, *The Theory of Economic Development* (Cambridge, MA: Harvard University Press, 1934).
4. Mark S. Granovetter, "The Strength of Weak Ties," *American Journal of Sociology*, vol. 78, no. 6 (1973), pp. 1360–1380.
5. Morten T. Hansen, "The Search-Transfer Problem: The Role of Weak Ties in Sharing Knowledge Across Organization Subunits," *Administrative Science Quarterly*, vol. 44, no. 1 (1999), pp. 82–111; Zeki Ozdemir, Peter Moran, Xing Zhong and Martin J. Bliemel, "Reaching and Acquiring Valuable Resources: The Entrepreneur's Use of Brokerage, Cohesion, and Embeddedness," *Entrepreneurship Theory and Practice*, vol. 40, no. 1 (2016), pp. 49–79; Ray Reagans and Bill McEvily, "Network Structure and Knowledge Transfer: The Effects of Cohesion and Range," *Administrative Science Quarterly*, vol. 48, no. 2 (2003), pp. 240–267.
6. Balagopal Vissa, "Agency in Action: Entrepreneurs' Networking Style and Initiation of Economic Exchange," *Organization Science*, vol. 23, no. 2 (2012), pp. 492–510.

7. Claudia Smith, J. Brock Smith and Eleanor Shaw, "Embracing Digital Networks: Entrepreneurs' Social Capital Online," *Journal of Business Venturing*, vol. 32, no. 1 (2017), pp. 18–34.
8. Eileen Fischer and A. Rebecca Reuber, "Social Interaction via New Social Media: (How) Can Interactions on Twitter Affect Effectual Thinking and Behavior?" *Journal of Business Venturing*, vol. 26, no. 1 (2011), pp. 1–18; Eileen Fischer and A. Rebecca Reuber, "Online Entrepreneurial Communication: Mitigating Uncertainty and Increasing Differentiation via Twitter," *Journal of Business Venturing*, vol. 29, no. 4 (2014), pp. 565–583.
9. Ozdemir et al. (2016).
10. Howard E. Aldrich and Phillip H. Kim, "Small Worlds, Infinite Possibilities? How Social Networks Affect Entrepreneurial Team Formation and Search," *Strategic Entrepreneurship Journal*, vol. 1, no. 1–2 (2007), pp. 147–165.
11. Ozdemir et al. (2016); Neha Parikh Shah, Rob Cross and Daniel Z. Levin, "Performance Benefits from Providing Assistance in Networks: Relationships That Generate Learning," *Journal of Management*, vol. 44, no. 2, 412–444.
12. Ibid.
13. Fischer and Reuber (2011).
14. Ibid.
15. Ibid.
16. Fischer and Reuber (2014).
17. Lee and Jones (2008).
18. Smith et al. (2017).

CHAPTER 12

Experiment with Self-Identities; Don't Be Rigidly Defined by Them

How entrepreneurs from marginalized and minority groups view themselves in various situations can considerably influence how well they develop and grow their ventures. When they exhibit a strong collective identity orientation, they are likely to develop ventures that primarily cater to the needs of their communities, and embrace both social and economic objectives.[1] However, their ventures will eventually run out of steam as competition intensifies for the same pool of resources, employees and customers. In line with our previous discussion, this implies that their prospects for growth, profitability and survival depend on their degree of participation in mainstream markets.

This brings us back to previous concerns about their ability to effectively operate in these markets. Research points to serious challenges. For example, when deciding how much to pay for novel products, there is evidence that mainstream consumers exhibit stereotype-induced bias.[2] Specifically, they perceive the quality of novel products offered by minority entrepreneurs (i.e., black entrepreneurs) to be lower than comparable products offered by their traditionally dominant (white) peers. They are also doubtful that minority entrepreneurs are interested in serving the larger marketplace, as opposed to their communities. All of this translates into less demand for minority entrepreneurs' products in mainstream markets. Furthermore, they are forced to sell even high-quality products at a discount. This can result in money-losing operations that prematurely put them out of business.

This observation reinforces the view that it can be difficult for minority entrepreneurs to concurrently navigate their communities and mainstream markets. To be sure, they will find it particularly difficult when they rigidly define themselves as members of a particular group or community. When they do so, they can inadvertently undermine their entrepreneurial efforts and outcomes by making it more difficult for them to keep their need for belonging and need for distinctiveness in balance.[3] Compared with entrepreneurs from traditionally dominant groups, those from marginalized and minority ones have to pursue a delicate balance by concurrently participating in communities and mainstream markets that are culturally and economically different.

When operating in their own communities, a stronger collective identity orientation could mean stronger social ties, greater sense of belonging, and higher levels of self-worth.[4] Recent immigrant or refugee entrepreneurs are particularly likely to value these group- or community-based psychosocial benefits when trying to settle in their newly adopted countries. Black entrepreneurs may similarly value these benefits. Still, they all have to satisfy their need for distinctiveness, while facing the possibility that mainstream players may not see them as they wish to be viewed.

A strong and rigid collective identity orientation will generally make it difficult for them to address these issues. In particular, it can hold back marginalized and minority entrepreneurs by making it hard for them to address misalignments between their desired image (how they want others to perceive them) and their perceived image (how they think others perceive them).[5] For example, a woman entrepreneur who strongly identifies with women as a group may incorporate a collective identity orientation in her desired image as follows: "I'm a competent and likeable woman technology entrepreneur." Now, suppose she is at an early stage of engagement with high-status mainstream players (e.g., private equity investors or senior executives of Fortune 500 companies), and think that they hold negative stereotypes about women as entrepreneurs. In this case, her perceived image could be: (a) "She is warm, but incompetent at leading technology ventures," (b) "She is cold, but competent at leading technology ventures," or (c) "She is cold and incompetent at leading technology ventures."

We can easily capture similar cases with entrepreneurs from other negatively stereotyped marginalized groups by replacing "woman entrepreneur," with "black woman entrepreneur," "immigrant entrepreneur," "refugee entrepreneur," "Hispanic entrepreneur," among others; and appropriately restating the previous statements for desired image and perceived image. The more general point is that these cases present scenarios in which there is a negative image discrepancy—that is, the perceived image is less favorable than the desired image—at an early stage of a potential business relationship.[6] This can hurt marginalized and minority entrepreneurs in psychological, social, financial and physical terms.

Their psychological well-being will decline because their perceived image conveys that powerful mainstream players devalue a very important collective aspect of their self-identity, as reflected in their desired image.[7] They will also be socially worse off because these potential business partners might be reluctant to endorse them. This in turn will make it difficult for them to mobilize critical resources, attract reputable partners, and build their customer base. If so, they could be forced to prematurely close down their business, and suffer substantial financial losses.[8] The combined effects of these adverse outcomes could mean a decline in their mental and physical health.[9]

For these reasons, they need to address negative image discrepancies in one way or another. For example, they may keep a desired image that embodies a strong collective identity linked to their negatively stereotyped group. They may be motivated to do so because they feel a strong sense of belonging and pride. Perhaps they also think it is their moral responsibility to raise their community's profile in mainstream society. When making such decisions, they may very well know that impression management tactics offer another way forward. For example, they could downplay the collective aspect of their self-identity and desired image by drawing more attention to their individual accomplishments. In addition, they could get influential mainstream players to see them as likeable by appropriately deploying ingratiation tactics.

Although these impression management tactics can be helpful, they may take a pass on them. They may specifically do so if they experience psychological discomfort from what they perceive as a lack of authenticity; that is, a misrepresentation of the lived experiences, values, beliefs, feelings, needs or wants that truly define them.[10] At the same time, they may try to improve their perceived image by courteously educating potential industry partners about the drawbacks of stereotypes.[11] In addition, they may share positive attributes about their group or community.

Although promising, this approach is unlikely to help marginalized and minority entrepreneurs get ahead when they are just starting out in mainstream markets. At this early stage, they are yet to prove themselves and establish a stellar track record. Therefore, they are significantly disadvantaged by a negative perceived image in the eyes of leading mainstream players. A key focus should be on getting these potential business partners to view them in a positive light from the very first interaction. They would certainly help their cause by projecting an image that portrays them as reasonably confident, competent, credible and likeable innovators. They can nail this positive perceived image by appropriately deploying the impression management tactics we previously discussed.

Going one step further, they stand to gain more from a personal or relational identity orientation than a collective identity orientation at an early stage of business development in mainstream markets. In particular, the former two identity orientations can help them better convince skeptical business partners to take a chance on them. After all, they would be primarily focused on their distinctive personal or relational qualities—that is, accomplishments, business acumen, qualifications, interpersonal skills, partnership role and so on—that signal their high potential to succeed as entrepreneurs. If they go on to land a deal (i.e., raise funds from private equity investors, or sign a leading corporate client), the next key task is to convert their positive perceive image in a strong personal brand by progressively building a track record of success.

Interestingly, some of the most successful minority executives in corporate America have apparently followed this approach. There is evidence that they normally start out at their firms under more pressure than their white peers to prove themselves.[12] This is certainly unfair and shouldn't happen. But minority executives who take up this challenge usually fare better than those who don't. Specifically, the former gain an enduring advantage by first projecting a positive image, and subsequently proving themselves. In response, their superiors reward them through higher pay, and promotion into senior management roles.

All these observations and arguments are consistent with the view that minority entrepreneurs and their fledging ventures can fare better in mainstream markets when they define themselves in less rigid ways. I previously emphasized the merit of a strategic identity orientation. This identity orientation is premised on a reasonably flexible view of one's self, particularly as one navigates different social contexts. In addition, marginalized and minority entrepreneurs need to take a flexible approach to identity orientation over time.

As their ventures grow, they will need to redefine themselves because their ability to continuously mobilize resources and conduct business depends on how well they meet the diverse and changing expectations of an evolving cast of stakeholders—from relatives, friends, co-founders, government grant agencies and private equity investors in the earlier stages to employees, suppliers, customers, bankers, shareholders, stock market analysts, industry experts or critics, outside directors, regulators, activist groups, among others, in the later stages.[13] More generally, they need to recognize that they are operating in a hypercompetitive and dynamic global marketplace, buffeted by disruptive technologies and other unexpected external forces. These forces can compound the pressure on them to redefine themselves and adapt.

A major concern is that they may inadvertently hold back themselves by changing how they view themselves much slower than they should. Like entrepreneurs from dominant groups, their self-identities will generally change slowly because of how they view themselves in the past versus the future.[14] Specifically, they think who they are today is who they'll be tomorrow, even when they already know that who they are today is different from who they were yesterday. In other words, they are much better at recognizing who they've been in the past than anticipating who they'll become in the future.

Going beyond this general impediment to change, marginalized and minority entrepreneurs are specifically pushed and pulled toward a collective identity orientation. They are very likely to enact and sustain a collective identity orientation because it is more salient than either a personal or relational (role-based) identity orientation. This happens because they are constantly bombarded by information cues—including negative stereotypes, minority status, and self-identification requests—that make them more attentive to their group affiliation than they otherwise would be. This implies that they will change how they view themselves much slower than their peers from traditionally dominant groups (i.e., white male entrepreneurs).

All of this means that immigrants, refugees, women, blacks, Asians, Hispanics and other marginalized enterprising individuals have a lot to think about when entering mainstream markets. From one situation, or time, to another, they have to diligently monitor their desired and perceived images as they try to court key stakeholders, mobilize resources and attract customers in such markets. They should consider addressing gaps between these images, and inadequacies in both, by deploying appropriate impression management tactics.[15]

More generally, they need to recognize and proactively manage their multiple self-identities. They are in a better position to effectively do so if they go beyond a narrow view of authenticity that confines them to a comfortable, but limiting view of their "real" or "true" selves.[16] In the spirit of innovation, what counts as authentic or genuine are the new versions of themselves that they create from viewing themselves in new ways, and what they imagine or admire in others.[17]

Furthermore, since they have multiple potential selves to explore, it would be premature and unwise to quickly cling to even the most comforting self-conception as their true self. Instead, they should reflectively experiment with different trial versions of themselves. In doing so, they can receive helpful feedback from others.

Building on such feedback, they can go on to refine and enact the most enabling future versions of themselves for various settings and times.

NOTES

1. Gry Agnete Alsos, Tommy Høyvarde Clausen, Ulla Hytti and Sølvi Solvoll, "Entrepreneurs' Social Identity and the Preference of Causal and Effectual Behaviours in Start-Up Processes," *Entrepreneurship and Regional Development*, vol. 28, no. 3–4 (2016), pp. 234–258; Jason Lortie, Gary J. Castrogiovanni and Kevin C. Cox, "Gender, Social Salience, and Social Performance: How Women Pursue and Perform in Social Ventures," *Entrepreneurship & Regional Development*, vol. 29, no. 1–2 (2017), pp. 155–173; Isaac H. Smith and Warner P. Woodworth, "Developing Social Entrepreneurs and Social Innovators: A Social Identity and Self-Efficacy Approach," *Academy of Management Learning & Education*, vol. 11, no. 3 (2012), pp. 390–407.
2. Peter Younkin and Venkat Kuppuswamy, "Discounted: The Effect of Founder Race on the Price of New Products," *Journal of Business Venturing*, vol. 34, no. 2 (2019), pp. 389–412.
3. Shepherd and Patzelt (2018).
4. Brickson (2000); Roberts (2005).
5. Roberts (2000).
6. The concept of image discrepancy is discussed in greater detail in Roberts (2000).
7. This point is grounded in insights from the following sources: by Manfred F. R. Kets de Vries, "The Dark Side of Entrepreneurship," *Harvard Business Review*, vol. 85, no. 6 (1985), 160–167; Shepherd and Patzelt (2018).
8. Deniz Ucbasaran, Dean A. Shepherd, Andy Lockett and S. John Lyon, "Life After Business Failure: The Process and Consequences of Business Failure for Entrepreneurs," *Journal of Management*, vol. 39, no. 1 (2013), pp. 163–202.

9. Ucbasaran et al. (2013).
10. Susan Harter, "Authenticity," in C R. Snyder and Shane J. Lopez, eds., *Handbook of Positive Psychology* (New York: Oxford University Press, 2002), pp. 382–394; Herminia Ibarra, "Provisional Selves: Experimenting with Image and Identity in Professional Adaptation," *Administrative Science Quarterly*, vol. 44, no. 4 (1999), pp. 764–791; Roberts (2005).
11. Roberts (2005).
12. Thomas and Gabarro (1999).
13. Mary J. Benner, "Securities Analysts and Incumbent Response to Radical Technological Change: Evidence from Digital Photography and Internet Telephony," *Organization Science*, vol. 21, no. 1 (2010), pp. 42–62; Peter Boatwright, Suman Basuroy and Wagner Kamakura, "Reviewing the Reviewers: The Impact of Individual Film Critics on Box Office Performance," *Quantitative Marketing and Economics*, vol. 5, no. 4 (2007), pp. 401–425; Greg Fisher, Suresh Kotha and Amrita Lahiri, "Changing with the Times: An Integrated View of Identity, Legitimacy, and New Venture Life Cycles," *Academy of Management Review*, vol. 41, no. 3 (2016), pp. 383–409; Lubomir P. Litov, Patrick Moreton and Todd R. Zenger, "Corporate Strategy, Analyst Coverage, and the Uniqueness Paradox," *Management Science*, vol. 58, no. 10 (2012), pp. 1797–1815.
14. Jordi Quoidbach, Daniel T. Gilbert and Timothy D. Wilson, "The End of History Illusion," *Science*, vol. 339, no. 6115 (2013), pp. 96–98.
15. Balachandra et al. (2019); Parhankangas and Ehrlich (2014).
16. Ibarra (1999); Herminia Ibarra, "The Authenticity Paradox," *Harvard Business Review*, vol. 93, no. 1–2 (2015), pp. 52–59.
17. Ibarra (2015).

CHAPTER 13

Strategically Accumulate Power and Appropriately Use It

An important observation is that entrepreneurs from marginalized and minority groups will fare better when they are politically skilled. On the surface, this basic insight suggests that they need to hone their political skills. On a deeper level, they should interpret it as a call to strategically accumulate power, and appropriately use it to their advantage. By power, I specifically mean their ability to advance their personal or business interests by influencing how others think, feel or behave on the one hand; and overcoming the constraining influence of others on the other hand.[1] In other words, they need to concurrently gain sufficient power over other people, and sufficient freedom from the power of other people.[2]

Given their initially disadvantaged socioeconomic position, many minority entrepreneurs generally start out with less power than entrepreneurs from traditionally dominant groups. In particular, they have less freedom from well-connected and powerful people in mainstream markets, and even within their own communities. This is primarily a reflection of their excessive dependence on others for access to valuable know-how, funding, legitimacy, and other complementary resources.[3] A major concern is that they might struggle, or prematurely fail, simply because powerful players—that is, business angel investors, or venture capital firms—withhold critical resources (i.e., funds, advice and connections) from them, or provide access to such resources on unfavorable terms—such as, demanding an exceptionally large equity stake in their ventures for a small amount of funds.

Powerful industry leaders can undermine entrepreneurs from marginalized and minority groups even when they don't intentionally withhold critical resources from them, or force them to accept bad deals. A less obvious aspect of their power is the ability to control or regulate the attention of almost everyone—from their peers, aspiring entrepreneurs, rivals, journalists, to politicians.[4] Oftentimes, those who are subject to this subtle form of power are unaware of its hold on them.[5] But when enterprising individuals from traditionally dominant groups exercise this kind of power, they effectively set the agenda (or rules of the game) that governs innovation on a national, or even international level.

In particular, they can define what challenges, problems or threats deserve the most attention; and what opportunities or solutions are worth pursuing. For example, CEOs from the prestigious club of Fortune 500 companies do so when they use various online and offline communication channels to selectively draw attention to technologies, such as artificial intelligence and machine learning, cloud computing, mobile computing, and the internet of things.[6] When they do so, the media, entrepreneurs, investors, academic researchers, companies, policymakers, among others, will become more attentive to the challenges and opportunities that these technologies present.

When this happens, private equity investors, corporations, universities and governments will prioritize such challenges and opportunities when making investment decisions, or fostering innovation or entrepreneurial ecosystems[7]; lawmakers will be motivated to enact new laws or regulations—that is, enforcing intellectual property rights—or strike down existing ones—that is, relaxing restrictive visa requirements for foreign-born knowledge workers or entrepreneurs—to deal with new challenges and promote job-creating opportunities[8]; and large corporations (i.e., Apple or Google) will reposition themselves to lead emerging innovation ecosystems.[9]

These and other developments are manifestations of the pervasive power of some mainstream industry leaders—well beyond the resources under their direct control; or the boundaries of their organizations, interpersonal relationships and interorganizational partnerships. They can set the innovation agenda in ways that affect how diverse stakeholders think; and consequently, whether they promote or inhibit some forms of innovation. When Apple displaced BlackBerry as a smartphone leader, it had exercised its power to set the innovation agenda for the smartphone industry. It later consolidated its dominant position by leading a growing network of independent software developers that are attentive to the opportunities that emanate from its iOs platform.

Entrepreneurs from marginalized and minority groups have to do the best they can, given the prevailing national or international innovation agenda before them. In particular, it makes sense for them to predominantly focus on continuously improving the terms under which they socially interact and conduct business with more powerful mainstream players (i.e., investors, suppliers, customers, or industry collaborators). Specifically, they need to find ways to improve, or offset, their relatively weak bargaining power when dealing with these players. The levers of power within their reach primarily embody personal qualities that help them attract powerful players, and credibly show that they offer unique value.

These personal qualities can help them get better outcomes by improving their bargaining power in two ways. The first way is by reducing their dependence on powerful parties. They can accomplish this by creating attractive outside options. In today's technology-driven global marketplace, they can do so by credibly signaling their technical competence as innovators. Specifically, they can attract multiple industry partners when they demonstrate their competence in core technological areas—possibly by successfully filing for patents associated with software security, cloud computing, computer vision, machine learning, virtual reality, autonomous driving, or drones, among other emerging technologies.[10] In this case, they will have several attractive outside options because multiple parties will try to outbid each other to acquire their valuable technical expertise and patents.[11]

For example, they can raise funds from multiple private equity investors on favorable terms, and go on to develop a product that uses their patents. They can also form partnerships with reputable corporations—including Amazon, Apple, Facebook, Google, IBM, Microsoft, Sony and Canon—and jointly develop globally distributed products and services that use their patents. Alternatively, they can generate revenue upfront by selling their patents to these corporations under an appropriate licensing agreement. Altogether, they have a relatively strong bargaining power because they are not dependent on any single party. Furthermore, they can credibly demand or hold out for better counteroffers, given their attractive outside options.

But even if there were few parties competing for their technical expertise and patents, they can still use their personal qualities to improve their bargaining power. This brings us to the second way in which such qualities can be power-enhancing for marginalized entrepreneurs: by making a dominant party refrain from exercising its power against them.

In keeping with the previous discussion, socially and politically skilled marginalized entrepreneurs can cultivate mutually beneficial partnerships with a dominant partner. They can specifically do so by deploying impression management tactics that consistently project them as reasonably confident, competent, credible and likeable innovators. Their positive image is likely to be validated when they own valuable intangible assets, or elicit admiration from their dominant partner. In this case, they can fare particularly well by effectively getting this partner to refrain from exercising its power against them. For example, investors from a dominant business angel network might go out their way to court and support a black female entrepreneur who is charismatic, or owns a patent for a new software security application.

Many marginalized entrepreneurs will not own a valuable patent. However, the same guiding principles apply when they are trying to bolster their initially limited power in social and business relationships. These relationships can be thought of as bargaining situations. By this I mean, they can come about because there is a common desire to cooperate and realize mutually satisfactory benefits. However, standing in the way are power imbalances, and/or conflicting interests, that often work in favor of parties from traditionally dominant groups.[12]

These bargaining situations are generally challenging for entrepreneurs from marginalized and minority groups, and particularly when they are necessity entrepreneurs—like recent immigrant or refugee IT professionals who cannot find acceptable work in their new host country; or native-born, highly qualified, black women who have been constantly passed over for promotion at Fortune 500 companies, among others. In keeping with our previous discussion, necessity entrepreneurs come to their ventures less prepared, and less resourced than others; and hence, more likely to find themselves excessively dependent on others for critical resources. As a result, they are even less free from the constraining influence of others within their own communities, and mainstream society.

But rather than passively approach, or walk away from, bargaining situations in their social and business affairs, marginalized and minority entrepreneurs should embrace and actively manage them. They can fair relatively well in their dealings with dominant mainstream parties when they strategically bolster their bargaining power and effectively negotiate. As previously shown, their complementary social and political skills will particularly serve them well in this case. It is worth emphasizing that they can make substantial progress in difficult bargaining situations by approaching more powerful parties in a reasonably confident way; and ultimately, by credibly showing that they are competent at something that such parties value.

NOTES

1. Ernst Fehr, Holger Herz and Tom Wilkening, "The Lure of Authority: Motivation and Incentive Effects of Power," *American Economic Review*, vol. 103, no. 4 (2013), pp. 1325–1359; Rachel E. Sturm and John Antonakis, "Interpersonal Power: A Review, Critique, and Research Agenda," *Journal of Management*, vol. 41, no. 1 (2015), pp. 136–163.
2. This point is primarily inspired by the view of power described in this work: Joris Lammers, Janka I. Stoker and Diederik A. Stapel, "Differentiating Social and Personal Power: Opposite Effects on Stereotyping, but Parallel Effects on Behavioral Approach Tendencies," *Psychological Science*, vol. 20, no. 12 (2009), pp. 1543–1548.
3. Richard M. Emerson, "Power-Dependence Relations," *American Sociological Review*, vol. 27, no. 1 (1962), pp. 31–40.
4. The following sources speak to the potential for powerful people to have pervasive influences that go beyond their intentional control of resources: John J. R. French, Jr., and Bertram Raven, "The Bases of Social Power," in Dorwin Cartwright, ed., *Studies in Social Power* (Ann Arbor: University of Michigan, 1959), pp. 150–167; Sturm and Antonakis (2015).
5. Ibid.
6. Alan Murray, "Fortune 500 CEOs See A.I. as a Big Challenge," *Fortune* (June 8, 2017).
7. Gary Dushnitsky, "Corporate Venture Capital in the 21st Century: An Integral Part of Firms' Innovation Toolkit," in Douglas Cumming, ed., *Oxford Handbook of Venture Capital* (New York: Oxford University Press, 2012), pp. 156–210; Gary Dushnitsky and Michael J. Lenox, "When Does Corporate Venture Capital Investment Create Firm Value?" *Journal of Business Venturing*, vol. 21, no. 6 (2006), pp. 753–772; Iain Klugman and Kevin Lynch, "Toronto-Waterloo corridor could be Canada's own Silicon Valley," *The Globe and Mail* (October 13, 2015); Christos Kolympiris and Peter G. Klein, "The Effects of Academic Incubators on University Innovation," *Strategic Entrepreneurship Journal*, vol. 11, no. 2 (2017), pp. 145–170; Gideon D. Markman, Phillip H. Phan, David B. Balkin and Peter T. Gianiodis, "Entrepreneurship and University-Based Technology Transfer," *Journal of Business Venturing*, vol. 20, no. 2 (2005), pp. 241–

263; Josh Lerner, "The Future of Public Efforts to Boost Entrepreneurship and Venture Capital," *Small Business Economics*, vol. 35, no. 3 (2010), pp. 255–264; OECD, *High-Growth Enterprises: What Governments Can Do to Make a Difference?* (Paris: OECD, 2010); Sean Silcoff, "Funding Set to Flow to Five Superclusters as Part of Ottawa's $950-Million Initiative," *The Globe and Mail* (November 12, 2018); Ben Spigel, "The Relational Organization of Entrepreneurial Ecosystems," *Entrepreneurship Theory and Practice*, vol. 41, no. 1 (2017), pp. 49–72.
8. Julien Chaisse and Xinjie Luan, "Revisiting the Intellectual Property Dilemma: How Did We Get to a Strong WTO IPR Regime?," *Santa Clara High Technology Law Journal*, vol. 34, no. 2 (2018), pp. 153–178; Clemente Forero-Pineda, "The Impact of Stronger Intellectual Property Rights on Science and Technology in Developing Countries," *Research Policy*, vol. 35, no. 6 (2006), pp. 808–824; Richard Florida and Ian Hathaway, "Solving Canada's Startup Dilemma," *The Globe and Mail* (November 2, 2018); Nancy T. Gallini, "The Economics of Patents: Lessons from Recent U.S. Patent Reform," *Journal of Economic Perspectives*, vol. 16, no. 2 (2002), pp. 131–154; Tracey Lindeman, "Canada Launches Visa Program for Hiring Specialized Foreign Talent," *The Globe and Mail* (June 13, 2017); Randall Palmer, "Canada Designs New Visa for Immigrant Entrepreneurs," *The Globe and Mail* (September 11, 2012).
9. R. Duane Ireland, Jeffrey G. Covin and Donald F. Kuratko, "Conceptualizing Corporate Entrepreneurship Strategy," *Entrepreneurship Theory and Practice*, vol. 33, no. 1 (2009), pp. 19–46; Martin Kornberger, "The Visible Hand and the Crowd: Analyzing Organization Design in Distributed Innovation Systems," *Strategic Organization*, vol. 15, no. 2 (2017), pp. 174–193; Arun Kumaraswamy, Raghu Garud and Shahzad (Shaz) Ansari, "Perspectives on Disruptive Innovations," *Journal of Management Studies*, vol. 55, no. 7 (2018), pp. 1025–1042; Satish Nambisan, "Digital Entrepreneurship: Toward a Digital Technology Perspective of Entrepreneurship," *Entrepreneurship Theory and Practice*, vol. 41, no. 6 (2017), pp. 1029–1055.
10. Knut Blind, Jakob Edler, Rainer Frietsch and Ulrich Schmoch, "Motives to Patent: Empirical Evidence from Germany," *Research Policy*, vol. 35, no. 5 (2006), pp. 655–672; Seth Fiegerman, "In Tech, Patents Are Trophies—And These Companies Are Dominating," *CNN* (June 19, 2018); Michael Webb, Nick Short, Nicholas Bloom and Josh Lerner, "Some Facts of High-Tech Patenting," NBER Working Paper No. 24793, July 2018.
11. The following sources more comprehensively cover the various commercialization and partnership (i.e., backing from venture capital investors) options that are available for exploiting or monetizing intellectual property rights such as patents: Iain M. Cockburn and Megan J. MacGarvie,

"Patents, Thickets and the Financing of Early-Stage Firms: Evidence from the Software Industry," *Journal of Economics & Management Strategy*, vol. 18, no. 3 (2009), pp. 729–773; Dirk Engel and Max Keilbach, "Firm-level Implications of Early Stage Venture Capital Investment—An Empirical Investigation," *Journal of Empirical Finance*, vol. 14, no. 2 (2007), pp. 150–167; Gaétan de Rassenfosse, "How SMEs Exploit Their Intellectual Property Assets: Evidence from Survey Data," *Small Business Economics*, vol. 39, no. 2 (2012), pp. 437–452; Sharon D. James, Michael J. Leiblein and Shaohua Lu, "How Firms Capture Value from Their Innovations," *Journal of Management*, vol. 39, no. 5 (2013), pp. 1123–1155; Joshua S. Gans and Scott Stern, "The Product Market and the Market for 'Ideas': Commercialization Strategies for Technology Entrepreneurs," *Research Policy*, vol. 32, no. 2, pp. 333–350; Noni Symeonidoua, Johan Bruneel and Erkko Autio, "Commercialization Strategy and Internationalization Outcomes in Technology-Based New Ventures," *Journal of Business Venturing*, vol. 32, no. 3 (2017), pp. 302–317.

12. Abhinay Muthoo, *Bargaining Theory with Applications* (Cambridge: Cambridge University Press, 1999); Abhinay Muthoo, "A Non-Technical Introduction to Bargaining Theory," *World Economics*, vol. 1, no. 2 (2000), pp. 145–166.

CHAPTER 14

Strategically Target and Use Government Support

As previously argued and illustrated, marginalized and minority entrepreneurs can overcome the challenges associated with the outsider problem when they cultivate enabling personal qualities and strategies. But many will struggle to do so, or outrightly fail, even when they are doing their best. The good news is that help is on the way.

In advanced developed countries (i.e., the United States, Canada and Britain), there is a variety of government-sponsored support programs that are generally aimed at new ventures and small- and medium-sized enterprises (SMEs)—officially defined in Canada as private sector, for-profit, companies with 1–499 employees and an annual revenue between $30,000 and $50 million.[1] The financial dimension of these support programs warrant special attention because the formal financial system generally underserves entrepreneurs, and particularly those from marginalized and minority groups.[2]

The Canadian banking system illustrates this situation. Since a few large banks (i.e., the "Big Six") dominate it,[3] entrepreneurs from these groups will generally find it difficult to get approved for business loans. One reason for this is that large banks are reluctant to lend to small business owners because they are not adequately compensated for the time commitment, transaction costs and risks associated with small business lending.[4] Furthermore, since these banks usually lack complete or reliable information about entrepreneurs and their companies, it can take substantial time and effort to assess their creditworthiness, compared with large or publicly traded companies.[5] In addition, it can be time-consuming to monitor small business loans. However, the adoption of credit scoring technologies has made it easier and cheaper for most large banks to meet the financing needs of new ventures and SMEs.[6]

Still, many minority owners will struggle to obtain bank loans because they are unable to meet the basic requirements for loan approval. In particular, their personal credit history and business track record may be below predetermined lending standards. In addition, they may lack the assets that banks value and normally accept as collateral—including cash, treasury bills, stocks, bonds, mutual funds, inventory, accounts receivable, or real estate property.

Innovative minority entrepreneurs are particularly likely to be turned down by banks. The fundamental problem is their risk profile.[7] Although research and development (R&D) intensive, or technology-based ventures can be innovative and lucrative operations, they are more prone to failure than established companies with proven products or services.[8] Furthermore, since their most valuable assets are in an intangible form— that is, knowledge embedded in experienced software engineers and senior executives—banks are unable to seize and sell these assets to recoup losses when they fail.[9]

But while an elevated risk profile will turn off banks, it can reel in private equity investors. In today's science- and technology-driven, global marketplace, getting support from these investors is critical for the growth and development of innovative new ventures. This support can come in the form of funding, strategic advice, management team development, connections, and endorsement or legitimacy. When innovative entrepreneurs from marginalized and minority groups lack this kind of support, they are likely to develop fewer science- or technology-based ventures than they can.[10] In addition, they will miss out on opportunities to develop global companies with reputable brands.[11]

Consider the case of women and immigrant entrepreneurs in Canada.[12] Research indicates that many women and immigrant entrepreneurs are motivated to develop and grow their ventures. They understand how important it is to introduce differentiated offerings with value-added features that are difficult, or costly for their competitors to imitate. More generally, they want to develop new, or significantly improved, products and services that meet the underserved needs of customers in the global marketplace. However, compared with their male and native-born counterparts, they struggle to globally expand their ventures because they are unable to meet the resource requirements of a globally oriented strategy.

Therefore, it is important to figure out whether and how marginalized and minority entrepreneurs can use government support to their advantage. If the primarily goal is to eventually win over private equity investors, research suggests that they should strategically target prestigious government grants.[13] There is evidence that they can credibly signal their technical competence and the quality of their ventures to these investors when they win such grants.[14]

They stand to gain a lot from leveraging prestigious government grants in countries where this pool of investors is growing under various public-private partnerships. For example, the Canadian government—that is, Export Development Canada (EDC)—has long provided guarantees for the loans that exporting SMEs seek from private and independently operated Canadian banks.[15] Building on this public-private partnership, the federal government—that is, Business Development Bank of Canada (BDC)—has been providing more funding opportunities for innovative entrepreneurs by co-investing with various groups of private equity investors (i.e., business angel networks, accelerators, or venture capital funds).

But since the Canadian government primarily wants to attract as many of these investors as possible, it has allowed its private equity partners to independently screen and select entrepreneurs and their ventures.[16] In the absence of socially motivated goals or political interference, entrepreneurs from traditionally disadvantaged groups will lack preferential access to the growing pool of venture capital. As a result, they will particularly benefit from winning government grants that private equity investors and other industry partners perceive as a "stamp of approval," or "symbol of quality."

When targeting prestigious government grants, they should also take advantage of complementary government-sponsored programs. In particular, they should prioritize programs that enable them to engage in mutually beneficial knowledge-sharing interactions with diverse entrepreneurs and business leaders.[17] In other words, they should capitalize on government-sponsored programs that facilitate social interaction, learning and capability development.

In keeping with our previous discussion, they should especially take advantage of government-sponsored training programs aimed at personal and professional development—including the cultivation of a growth mindset, and social and political skills.[18] They should also be alert to the wide array of export support programs that can help them conduct business in global markets in a more informed, safer and cheaper way.[19] There are also opportunities to sell goods and services to government departments that are worth pursuing.[20] When appropriately combined, these forms of government support can collectively help them succeed by removing, or at least by alleviating, barriers that can undermine even heroic individual effort.

As government policies and programs change over time, they should try to optimize the value of government support by actively scanning, targeting and leveraging government programs with the greatest potential to create follow-on, or future value (such as prestigious grants; programs geared toward personal and professional development). Going one step further, they should consider making the acquisition of prestigious government grant awards a key milestone—especially during the earlier stages of their ventures; when they are necessity entrepreneurs; or when they are affiliated with a group that is negatively stereotyped as lacking scientific, technological and/or entrepreneurial competence. They will set themselves up for long-term success when they take this calculative or strategic approach to government support.

Notes

1. Statistics Canada, *Survey on Financing and Growth of Small and Medium Enterprises, 2017*. Available online: https://www150.statcan.gc.ca/n1/daily-quotidien/181116/dq181116c-eng.htm (Accessed December 28, 2018).
2. Berger and Udell (1998); Berger et al. (1998, 2005); Steven N. Kaplan and Per Strömberg, "Venture Capitalists as Principals: Contracting, Screening, and Monitoring," *American Economic Review*, vol. 91, no. 2 (2001), pp. 426–430; Maula et al. (2005); OECD, *High-Growth Enterprises: What Governments Can Do to Make a Difference* (Paris: OECD Publishing, 2010); Shane and Cable (2002); Stein (2002).
3. Robert J. McKeown, "An Overview of the Canadian Banking System: 1996 to 2015," Queen's Economics Department Working Paper No. 1379, 2017.
4. Berger et al. (2005); Berger and Udell (1998); Stein (2002).
5. Ibid.
6. Allen N. Berger, W. Scott Frame and Nathan H. Miller, "Credit Scoring and the Availability, Price, and Risk of Small Business Credit," *Journal of Money, Credit and Banking*, vol. 37, no. 2 (2005), pp. 191–222; W. Scott Frame, Aruna Srinivasan and Lynn Woosley, "The Effect of Credit Scoring

on Small-Business Lending," *Journal of Money, Credit and Banking*, vol. 33, no. 3 (2001), pp. 813–825.
7. Bronwyn H. Hall and Josh Lerner, "The Financing of R&D and Innovation," in Bronwyn H. Hall and Nathan Rosenberg, eds., *Handbook of the Economics of Innovation*, vol. 1 (North Holland: Elsevier, 2010), pp. 609–639; Stephen Martin and John T. Scott, "The Nature of Innovation Market Failure and the Design of Public Support for Private Innovation," *Research Policy*, vol. 29, no. 4–5 (2000), pp. 437–447.
8. Ibid.
9. Ibid.
10. This point is consistent with the view that venture capital investors foster innovation in their portfolio firms. For example, see the following sources: James R. Brown, Steven M. Fazzari, and Bruce C. Petersen, "Financing Innovation and Growth: Cash Flow, External Equity, and the 1990s R&D Boom," *Journal of Finance*, vol. 64, no. 1 (2009), pp. 151–185; Samuel Kortum and Josh Lerner, "Assessing the Contribution of Venture Capital to Innovation," *RAND Journal of Economics*, vol. 31, no. 4 (2000), pp. 674–692; Jeffry A. Timmons and William D. Bygrave, "Venture Capital's Role in Financing Innovation for Economic Growth," *Journal of Business Venturing*, vol. 1, no. 2 (1986), pp. 161–176.
11. Stephanie A. Fernhaber and Patricia P. McDougall-Covin, "Venture Capitalists as Catalysts to New Venture Internationalization: The Impact of Their Knowledge and Reputation Resources," *Entrepreneurship Theory and Practice*, vol. 33, no. 1 (2009), pp. 277–295.
12. This section draws on the following sources: Clare Beckton, Janice McDonald and Maude Marquis-Bissonnette, *Everywhere, Every Day Innovating: Women Entrepreneurs and Innovation Report*, 2018. Available online: http://bmoforwomen.bmo.com/wp-content/uploads/2018/02/Everywhere_Everyday_Innovating_EN_Final.pdf (Accessed July 7, 2018); David Green, Huju Liu, Yuri Ostrovsky and Garnett Picot, *Immigration, Business Ownership and Employment in Canada* (Ottawa: Statistics Canada, Catalogue no. 11F0019M—No. 375, 2016); Horatio M. Morgan, Sui Sui and Mathias Baum, "Are SMEs with Immigrant Owners Exceptional Exporters?," *Journal of Business Venturing*, vol. 33, no. 3 (2018), pp. 241–260; François Neville, Barbara Orser, Allan Riding and Owen Jung, "Do Young Firms Owned by Recent Immigrants Outperform Other Young Firms?," *Journal of Business Venturing*, vol. 29, no. 1 (2014), pp. 55–71; Barbara Orser, Martine Spence, Allan Riding and Christine A. Carrington, "Gender and Export Propensity," *Entrepreneurship Theory and Practice*, vol. 34, no. 5 (2010), pp. 933–957; Martha A. Reavley, Terri Lituchy and Emma McClelland, "Exporting Success: A Two Country Comparison of Women Entrepreneurs in International Trade," *International Journal of Entrepreneurship and Small Business*, vol. 2, no. 1 (2005), pp. 57–78; Sui Sui

and Horatio M. Morgan, *Selling Beyond the U.S.: Do Recent Immigrants Advance Canada's Export Agenda?* (Ottawa: The Conference Board of Canada, 2014); Sui Sui, Horatio M. Morgan and Matthias Baum, "Internationalization of Immigrant-Owned SMEs: The Role of Language," *Journal of World Business*, vol. 50, no. 4 (2015), pp. 804–814.

13. This point is consistent with the insights and findings from the following research: Mazhar Islam, Adam Fremeth and Alfred Marcus, "Signaling by Early Stage Startups: US Government Research Grants and Venture Capital Funding," *Journal of Business Venturing*, vol. 33, no. 1 (2018), pp. 35–51; Michael Spence, "Job Market Signaling," *Quarterly Journal of Economics*, vol. 87, no. 3 (1973), pp. 355–374.
14. Ibid.
15. Vincent Chandler, "The Economic Impact of the Canada Small Business Financing Program," *Small Business Economics*, vol. 39, no. 1 (2012), pp. 253–264; Export Development Canada (EDC), Brochure: Export Guarantee Program. Available online: https://www.edc.ca/EN/Our-Solutions/Financing/Documents/brochure-export-guarantee-program.pdf (Accessed December 28, 2018).
16. Department of Finance Canada, *Backgrounder: Venture Capital and Angel Investment*. Available online: https://www.fin.gc.ca/n17/data/17-102_1-eng.asp (Accessed November 28, 2018).
17. Henrik Tötterman and Jan Sten, "Start-ups, Business Incubation and Social Capital," *International Small Business Journal*, vol. 23, no. 5 (2005), pp. 487–511.
18. Parhankangas and Ehrlich (2014); Fiona Wilson, Jill Kickul and Deborah Marlino, "Gender, Entrepreneurial Self-Efficacy, and Entrepreneurial Career Intentions: Implications for Entrepreneurship Education," *Entrepreneurship Theory and Practice*, vol. 31, no. 3 (2007), pp. 387–406.
19. Eileen Fischer and A. Rebecca Reuber, "Targeting Export Support to SMEs: Owners' International Experience as a Segmentation Basis," *Small Business Economics*, vol. 20, no. 1 (2003), pp. 69–82; Brendan J. Gray, "Profiling Managers to Improve Export Promotion Targeting," *Journal of International Business Studies*, vol. 28, no. 2 (1997), pp. 387–419.
20. Public Services and Procurement Canada, Help for Small and Medium Enterprises. Available online: https://www.tpsgc-pwgsc.gc.ca/app-acq/pme-sme/index-eng.html (Accessed December 29, 2018).

CHAPTER 15

Cultivate Higher-Order Mental Skills

As self-described underdog entrepreneurs, here's what marginalized and minority entrepreneurs need to understand: who they are and what they are becoming are shaped by everything that has happened to them, combined with the choices they have made at critical points in their life.

They have a personal history. This history includes the specific setbacks they have experienced because of costly, but avoidable mistakes. Some mistakes might reflect their lack of relevant know-how. Perhaps other mistakes happened because they lacked support from influential stakeholders, who consciously or unconsciously hold negative stereotypes about them. Their personal history also embodies how they have responded to disappointments along the way.

Perhaps their motivations changed after receiving yet another rejection letter: instead of being focused on what they want to achieve, they might have become more focused on things they want to get away from.

They might hold rigid beliefs about themselves, others and the world at large. These beliefs might have initially helped them cope with their setbacks. But now they have found themselves more socially isolated than they want to be. They are on the verge of giving up, having worked so hard and for so long.

But in those flickering moments when the sting of disappointments subsides, life presents them with opportunities for sweet reflection. They can enter into such moments when they begin to observe the underlying threads that connect their personal histories with those of others well beyond their own communities. When this happens, they may recognize the outsider problem as part of their common struggle.

This problem is particularly difficult to solve because it can induce counterproductive beliefs, feelings and behaviors. But the story does not have to end this way for marginalized and minority entrepreneurs. We now know that they can overcome this problem when they cultivate enabling personal qualities and strategies. But there's something else they need to know. They can give themselves an even better chance of achieving and sustaining success by cultivating metacognitive or higher-order mental skills.[1]

These skills are associated with a high level of mental self-awareness and mental adaptability under diverse circumstances. If marginalized and minority entrepreneurs are mentally self-aware, they will have an enhanced ability to think about how they are thinking when confronted with business-related tasks in new, complex, uncertain or dynamic situations.[2] The more mentally self-aware they are in these situations, the more appropriately they will respond to new challenges and opportunities. In other words, they will be mentally adaptive; that is, they can easily alter how they think about themselves, others, and larger external environment.

Another related higher-order mental skill is the ability to properly evaluate and formulate multiple approaches, or mental strategies, when dealing with different business or social situations.[3] When they have this ability, they will excel at thinking about their challenges, opportunities, tasks, others, and the world at large in the ways that enhance their chance of success. In addition, they will quickly figure out when a certain way of thinking about these issues no longer serves them well; and when they do, they are adept at adjusting their way of thinking. Building on these high-order mental skills, they can reach a higher level of metacognitive development when they excel at applying mental strategies that are most appropriate for the situation at hand.

The good news is that entrepreneurs from marginalized and minority groups can develop these higher-order mental skills through practice, professional training and meaningful social interactions.[4] With the help of trained practitioners, they can foster mental self-awareness by engaging in meaningful self-reflective exercises. Building on these exercises, they can improve their mental adaptability by actively deepening and broadening their knowledge base, experiences and perceptions. In doing so, they will expand the pool of mental resources and mental representations on which they can draw when confronted with new situations.

Importantly, they can also expand their repertoire of mental strategies by paying close attention to the strategies that business leaders apply in various situations. Even better, they should try to engage these leaders in a meaningful way when they have a chance to do so. Such interpersonal interactions can help them understand precisely why, how and when business leaders change their way of thinking in various situations.

Interestingly, traces of higher-order mental skills can be found in the business leaders' stories I have recounted. As initially disadvantaged individuals with a desire to succeed, Indra Nooyi, Jack Ma, Hilary Devey, and Mike Lazaridis all exhibit mental self-awareness, mental adaptability, and an enhanced ability to deploy situation-specific mental strategies. Such higher-order mental skills are reflected in their apparent growth mindset. They foster their own mental development by wanting to grow, and believing in their ability to do so. In addition to perceiving themselves in favorable ways, they also have an enabling view of the world: although it has difficult people and problems, one can win with an appropriate strategy and hard work.

Higher-order mental skills also come into play when these business leaders exhibit entrepreneurial alertness. When they scan their environment for new events or trends, their mental self-awareness will be activated as they try to make sense of an uncertain and complex world. They know that their prior knowledge and experience can serve as a guide when searching for information about such events or trends, or when they are trying to come up with a new business idea. Furthermore, they are able to spot opportunities that others overlook, or dismiss as too risky or difficult, because they deploy appropriate mental strategies to evaluate and exploit them.

Higher-order mental skills are also at work when business leaders exhibit a strategic identity orientation. When faced with the question "Who am I?" they understand why their answers reflect the meanings they attach to their communities, roles or personal qualities; as well as the meanings they attach to various social contexts or times. As a result, they are likely to envision a repertoire of self-identities on which they can draw, and enact the most suitable ones.

The high level of mental development achieved by consistently successful entrepreneurs sets a high bar for those who are weighed down by the outsider problem. But for self-described underdog entrepreneurs and others who are up for the challenge, there is good reason to be optimistic because they have viable pathways to success.

Notes

1. John J. Flavell, "Metacognition and Cognitive Monitoring: A New Area of Cognitive-Developmental Inquiry," *American Psychologist*, vol. 34, no. 10 (1979), pp. 906–911; Susan T. Fiske and Shelley E. Taylor, *Social Cognition*, 2nd ed. (New York, NY: McGraw-Hill Book Company, 1991); J. Michael Haynie, Dean Shepherd, Elaine Mosakowski and Christopher Earley, "A Situated Metacognitive Model of the Entrepreneurial Mindset," *Journal of Business Venturing*, vol. 25, no. 2 (2010), pp. 217–229; Thomas O. Nelson, "Consciousness and Metacognition," *American Psychologist*, vol. 51, no. 2 (1996), pp. 102–129.
2. Haynie et al. (2010).
3. Ibid.
4. Ibid.

CHAPTER 16

Conclusion: Underdog Entrepreneurs' Most Enduring Asset

As my mind drifts back to Wang Enlin in China, I see an aging farmer and self-taught lawyer locked in a legal battle with Qiqihar Chemical Group (QCG)—a powerful state-owned chemical company. No sooner had he won a legal victory than it started to slip away under the weight of QCG's appeal. When the court system ruled against Wang and his fellow villagers in the appeal process, it may have confirmed what they already knew.

"We're just farmers, without any resources or power … against the government, we can't win," said a villager from the senior citizen group that Wang had mobilized to protect the beauty and purity of Yushutun.[1]

Even without knowing where else to turn, Wang could have held his head high if he had walked away at this point. After all, he might have already taken more chances than he should. The local police had been watching him closely, and he knew it. In fact, they had warned him not to give interviews to the media during one of their regular visits to his house. But this advice went unheeded.

"In China, behind every case of pollution is a case of corruption," said Wang to a reporter.[2]

Now pressed to confront the grim prospects of losing an appeal he plans to file, the reporter and his friends might have expected to see him surrender. But they would have to wait another day.

Wang's response still resonates with me: "We will absolutely win. The law is on our side."[3] It's especially refreshing because no sooner had he spoken than a friend replied: "We may not even see justice in our lifetimes."[4]

Underdog entrepreneurs are hardly expected to turn to an aging and self-taught farmer-lawyer like Wang for advice. Yet, he might get them off to a good start. He might inspire them to keep trying; to never give up. But if they observe him closely, they might see that the greatest, and oftentimes, most enduring asset at the disposal of underdogs is what's in their heads.

When yet another setback breaks their hearts, thinking about themselves, others and the world at large in enabling ways can revitalize their resolve to transcend their underdog status. Their entrepreneurial journeys are unfolding on unleveled playing fields, and help sometime arrives almost too late.

But the good news is that they can make unexpected breakthroughs by cultivating the same code-breaking skills that have helped others succeed despite the odds.

Notes

1. Primary source of quote: NDTV, "Man Dropped Out of School, Taught Himself Law to Take on China's Largest Chemical Firm" (November 12, 2017).
2. Ibid.
3. Ibid.
4. Ibid.

CHAPTER 17

Epilogue: What Journey Brought Me Here?

As I stared at the blinking cursor on my blank Microsoft Word page, my eyes flickered and my mind went along with them.

Moments earlier, I had cleared several inches of snow from my driveway. Another load would undo my work minutes later. But I shrugged my shoulders and retreated in my cozy basement office.

I was in the mood to work on a research paper, but found myself being pulled away by imaginations well beyond my northern Greater Toronto Area (GTA) location.

The place was Jamaica, the island on which I was born and raised.

There I was, basking in its splendid sunshine with outstretched arms; being gently tossed around by a playful summer breeze.

From the balcony of a hotel in Negril, I took in a majestic view of a beach, decorated with glittery white sands and turquoise water. It didn't take long before I caved into its magnetic pull.

What started out as a timid step toward the edge of a rising wave became a plunge beneath it. I was about to ride another one that was coming my way, but the jarring sound of an alarm from my idle iPhone brought me back to a familiar place: work.

The next time my mind strayed, I didn't return to the island's pure paradise. Instead, I went to a part of Kingston that even the most adventurous Canadian-born tourist might have overlooked.

The place was Van Street.

That's where most of my early life unfolded.

© The Author(s) 2020
H. M. Morgan, *Underdog Entrepreneurs*,
https://doi.org/10.1007/978-3-030-20408-2_17

As my eyes scanned the 17 houses in the neighborhood, I remembered things. And smiled.

I saw myself playing a game of cricket with my buddies. But the game ended prematurely because someone's wildly swung bat sent a ball sailing through my neighbor's glass window. They scampered, leaving me to face my furious neighbor alone. Fortunately, she was unhurt, and I agreed to fix the damaged window pane.

The repair job was completed in less than three days. My neighbor was thrilled, but sternly warned me to be more careful next time. I agreed with a firm nod.

As one memory faded, another one replaced it.

I can see my father slithering half way under a raised Series VI Morris Oxford car. He was tinkering with the gearbox. I perhaps had more grease on my hands than he did; and certainly more than the other eight-year-old boys in the neighborhood. With my eyes set on a nearby tool box, I was ready to take his request for spanners, bolts and nuts in various sizes; plus an occasional request for water, or a glass of lemonade.

Moving away from this scene, I saw myself as a 14-year-old teenager. But the moment I arrived there, April 26, 1991, flashed before my eyes.

I didn't want to go back to this time; but that's where my thoughts lingered.

Even when my ears are sealed with the palm of my hands, I still hear the two sounds that would change my life forever: "Bang! ... Bang!"

Two gunmen had struck.

My dog, Crisis, was the first to go down in the line of duty.

Several years earlier, my dad brought her to our home all grown up. He called her Crisis. My sisters and I were so thrilled to receive her. When my dad confirmed that I would be the primary caregiver, I shuffled forward toward her on my knees with a smile and open arms. But she turned away and whined. With a gentle pat on her head, I tried to signal that she would be safe and happy with me. By end of the day, she was already groomed, fed and ready for a sweet sleep in the cozy bed I made for her. But she howled throughout the night.

Over the next few days, she would whine and turn away from the meals I prepared for her. I would later learn from my dad that Crisis was actually mourning because she had been separated from her four puppies. He had actually gotten Crisis from an owner who had wanted to give her away, but keep the puppies.

17 EPILOGUE: WHAT JOURNEY BROUGHT ME HERE? 153

Although my father had wanted all five of them from the very start, the owner wouldn't allow it. I'm still not sure what deal he struck, but I remember how elated I was when he returned with four beautiful puppies. A sweet reunion unfolded as they barked, danced and leaned into their mother. Joy had returned to her world, making me one of the happiest dog owners you could find at the time.

But on that fateful day when Crisis sought to protect the man who had rescued her, she would pay the ultimate sacrifice by taking the first of two bullets. Now lying motionless on the ground, she had become more than my lost friend: she had come to symbolize the crisis that had engulfed my life.

My father, Clifton Roy Morgan, age 47, went down with the second shot.

A spot I once swept to rid my yard of meddlesome leaves from a nearby mango tree was now watered with his blood.

I can still hear the revving of an engine as the gunmen escaped with his car and money. As the jarring sound fades, blurry images of my father and the life we once lived began to come into focus.

He was a man of faith with a cheerful and tender heart. I might have exhausted his patience with my worldly questions, desires and ambitions; but I'll never know for sure because there was no hint of frustration behind his seemingly constant smile.

His unending labor as a carpenter and taxi operator had often left him almost too sleepy to get through dinner. But his energy would magically return when it was time for us to have guitar-playing sessions. Sometimes these sessions morphed into reading and speaking practice sessions. Those were less fun because I was a slow reader at the time. But he would patiently wait for me to finish a paragraph or two from books that seemed difficult at the time. Once I got through that, the guitar-playing session resumed—he would remind me that we were still playing in the key of C, and that the chords were C-F-G.

Another thing he made time for was cooking.

On the days he joined my mother, Dorothy, in the kitchen, they would combine their imaginations and natural skills to transform basic ingredients—including sweet potatoes, yam, green banana, flour, cabbage, cod fish, and curry power—into delicious home-cooked meals.

My dad never actually said "I love you," but I always knew he did because his actions spoke louder than words ever could. During our music sessions, he told me that I belonged to a "royal family" and was destined for greatness. But to finally get there, he said I needed a "good education, not silver or gold." I didn't fully grasp what he meant then, but I believed him.

I was pulled from these sweeter memories against my will by an email notification that popped up on my computer. After responding to it, I was transported back to life in Canada.

It has been my adopted home country since Sharlene and I left Jamaica in September 2002 as newlyweds. One year earlier, I had convinced her that we needed to leave Jamaica for a fresh start. But when we received our Canadian permanent residence travel documents in April 2002, I had mixed emotions.

Despite the tragedy that had rocked my childhood, and fleeting moments of fear, I had had a splendid life in Jamaica.

As a teenager, I was particularly fortunate to receive parental support and guidance when it mattered most, and from the most generous people I've ever known. Like the couple Dennis V. Brown (former Partner, PricewaterhouseCoopers) and Grace Brown (restaurateur/business owner), who were simply "dad" and "mom" at the time.

Beyond offering me financial support, they helped me develop personally and professionally by setting goals (like preparing a 10-year career plan at 16 years old), maintaining high academic standards (treating "A−" as the minimum acceptable grade), learning on my own, and believing in my ability to accomplish great things. These qualities served me well during my high school and university years in Jamaica—Camperdown High School (grade 7–11) and Wolmer's Boys School (grades 12 and 13), where I specialized in the sciences (i.e., biology, chemistry and physics); and the University of the West Indies, Mona Campus, where I switched to the social sciences/business (i.e., economics and accounting).

Another part of this splendid life was my finance career that was set to take off in the Jamaican banking industry. The best part was the awesome friendships that I had at work and elsewhere. In fact, leaving my friends and mentors behind was the hardest part of leaving Jamaica.

But I had purchased one-way plane tickets for Toronto, and there was no turning back now. I remember scanning online neighborhood maps from Toronto to Hamilton. I contemplated potential obstacles that I could face as a finance professional in Canada. But nothing warranted special concern. Even with unanticipated setbacks, I expected to fully rebuild my life and career within five years.

17 EPILOGUE: WHAT JOURNEY BROUGHT ME HERE? 155

However, looking back at my first five years in Canada, I was far off my projections. Virtually all my expectations didn't materialize. It was considerably harder to settle, and rebuild my career than I could have imagined.

The first thing I struggled to come to terms with was that my credentials and work experience from Jamaica weren't worth much in Canada. But I was forced to deal with this reality because the hundreds of resumes I churned out during my first year didn't translate into job interviews at reputable companies, or government departments. I would later learn that I had lacked an elusive thing called "Canadian experience": Canadian companies apparently won't take a chance on newcomers if they lack it, but newcomers won't get it unless Canadian companies do so.

As my job search began to run out of steam, panic began to do its dirty work, separating the nuts and bolts that once held my neat life together. With no new income to tap up my dwindling savings, I had lacked a sturdy buffer against the tougher times I envisioned. I wasn't troubled too much by visions of hunger, because I had learned from my parents how to make a meal from virtually nothing. But fleeting thoughts of homelessness rattled me as the monthly rent cycle sucked in my savings.

Although joblessness and financial woes had taunted me, I was tormented by something far more serious: I was losing my desire to thrive in my new world. The mounting unfulfilled expectations and disappointments were beginning to break my spirit. The closest I had ever come to feeling this way was around the time of my father's untimely death. Yet even then, I had shown traces of an indomitable spirit—like the time I implored my sisters from a table top to lay claim on a prosperous future: "yesterday, we were an army without a country, but tomorrow we'll be looking for a country to buy. Let's march along, victory is ours!"

Now far removed from these naïve proclamations in Hamilton, Ontario, I was gradually being silenced by forces I didn't fully understand at the time. Not only was I talking less, I was also dreaming less too.

But before I retreated from the stage of life, I decided to try one last thing: move to a university campus and rebuild my life there. This wasn't an easy option because Sharlene and I were expecting our first child, and Canadian universities generally offer limited accommodations for families. But we were determined to give it a shot.

In 2004, we moved into campus residence at York University, Toronto, a month before I started the economics master's program. There I would meet professors Brenda Spotton Visano and Elie Appelbaum, who inspired me to go further in this field. So I was on my way to British Columbia to pursue doctoral studies in economics at Simon Fraser University in 2006. I was fortunate to have Professor Robert Jones (now retired) as my lead supervisor. Thanks to his seemingly boundless generosity, wisdom and advice, I was well-prepared to navigate academic and corporate life.

Shortly after completing my PhD, I returned to Toronto in 2010. Things turned out much better than I expected: I had a short stint at Grant Thornton (international taxation/transfer pricing practice) en route to an Assistant Professor (tenure track) position at the Ted Rogers School of Management, Ryerson University. Six years later, I was promoted to Associate Professor of Global Management. Since then, I have straddled industry, policy circles and academia.

The life-changing moments and amazing friends, colleagues and strangers I've met along the way are too numerous to mention here. But as a tenured business faculty at Ryerson University, I consider myself very fortunate to have an opportunity to do something I really love: actively explore and combine ideas from different fields (i.e., entrepreneurship, finance, economics, psychology and sociology) to conceive new perspectives or theories; and go on to develop, test and share them.

The thought of everyone having a chance to realize their full potential is very enticing to me. Based on my own experience, I was excited to start a research program on immigrants in Canada several years ago. Around that time, a dominant story was that immigrants were struggling as professionals and entrepreneurs. However, I wanted to know what immigrants were doing well, and what economic contributions they make to Canada. But such stories weren't forthcoming.

In 2014, my colleague (Sui Sui) and I teamed up with the Conference Board of Canada to fill this research gap. We provided substantial evidence that immigrant businesses can particularly contribute by helping Canada grow its exports in global markets.[1] Going one step further, our research team (with Matthias Baum) showed that immigrant entrepreneurs' enhanced ability to conduct business abroad is a reflection of their foreign language skills.[2] As it turns out, such language skills give immigrants a competitive edge when it comes to building and sustaining trusted business relationships in global markets. However, we've recently reported evidence that immigrant businesses export more than their Canadian-born peers, but earn less. We've shown that this disappointing result can occur because immigrants are more susceptible to overconfidence, and its negative effects, when making exporting decisions.[3]

17 EPILOGUE: WHAT JOURNEY BROUGHT ME HERE? 157

Although my research focused on comparable immigrant and Canadian-born entrepreneurs, there were important differences that deserved special attention. I was on a 1-year sabbatical (research leave) in 2017 when I started working toward a book that could shed light on such issues. Five years earlier, an economics conference had brought me to China for a week. While looking at notes and pictures from this trip in summer 2017, I was brought back in my mind to fascinating places, foods, music and people in China. All of this unfolded on a northward journey that started out in Southeast China, Guangzhou (Guangdong province); then Zhengzhou en route to Kaifeng (Henan province). I had hoped to return to China during my sabbatical, but ended up in Western Europe instead.

I visited Germany twice, moving between places such as Frankfurt, Mannheim, Hannover, Bremen and Osnabrück. In addition, I spent some time in the Netherlands—mainly in The Hague. Based on research, conferences and casual observations, I've had a good look at the challenges and opportunities that are before migrants and refugees in these countries. I'm thrilled to be part of an ongoing public discourse on how to strategically help them achieve better outcomes as professionals, and especially as entrepreneurs.

Based on the formidable challenges that newcomers face in rich countries, I found myself thinking about them as underdog professionals and entrepreneurs in a wide range of contests. My thoughts lingered on high-qualified immigrants who were forced to start a business because they couldn't find acceptable work. I was particularly concerned about their grim prospects in some cases. Eventually, I contemplated something that went beyond the lived experiences of immigrants. This would take me back to my own journey.

I imagined two distinct versions of myself: my current self, "older-Horatio," and my 14-year-old self, "younger-Horatio."

Older-Horatio is strong, yet sensitive. When he was transported back to Van Street on April 26, 1991, I imagined he saw younger-Horatio curled up in a corner with his hands crossed. Older-Horatio couldn't see the exact spot on the floor where his eyes were fixed, but he could hear his heavy, uneven breathing. Upon hearing the footsteps closing in, younger-Horatio started to raise his head. Still very much in need of his father, he might have thought those footsteps were his dad's. Besides, at 41, older-Horatio almost sounded and looked like his 47-old dad. So he could hardly tell the difference when older-Horatio whispered "son." They cried together and held each other tightly.

Moving away from this scene, another thought bubbled up to the surface. When we become successful, our lives can change in ways that make it difficult for us to identify with the pain, fear, despair, anger and even joy of those who are less fortunate. I don't immediately recognize the emotionally traumatized younger-Horatio when I look in the mirror. But he eventually appears if I stare long enough. The moment his past pain comes to the surface, we become one as I identify with him.

I've shared stories about enterprising and amazing people with whom I sense a connection, albeit from a distance. I remember being captivated by pictures of Wang Enlin sitting on his bed. I felt as if I was there, and wanted to know what had made him so sad. I saw pictures of the waste deposits that covered landscapes that were once natural and beautiful. I genuinely admire his courage, and want him to prevail in his legal battle. Such positive sentiments apply to others too.

Indra Nooyi strikes me as someone who is refreshingly open, honest and pragmatic. The moment she brought the idea of an "immigrant mentality," we were on the same page. Meanwhile, Jack Ma speaks to me when I observe his curiosity as a boy and his unwavering courage and energy throughout his life. When I look at Mike Lazaridis' life as an innovator and ardent supporter of education, it inspires me to take a chance on something much bigger than myself. And the grit of Hilary Devey reminds me of the power of the human spirit. I could go on about the other disadvantaged, yet bold and innovative entrepreneurs I've featured in this book. I imagine you've found someone with whom you could identify with.

For those who prefer hard evidence, I hope you discovered at least a bit of what you were looking for too. After all, I've developed and shared ideas based on evidence and insights from more than 300 peer-reviewed works spanning strategic management, entrepreneurship, economics, cognitive and social psychology, sociology, and entrepreneurial and small business finance. The copious notes that I've shared on relevant sources and ideas should also be helpful for diligent readers or researchers who want to dig deeper into various ideas or issues.

In closing, I hope this book is as revitalizing for you as you read it, as it was for me as I wrote it.

Notes

1. Sui and Morgan (2014).
2. Sui et al. (2015).
3. Morgan et al. (2018).

Index[1]

A
Aburaneh, Tahani, ix, 5
Acquisition(s), 1, 37, 47, 142
ADDIE & CO Solicitors, 11
Addo, Aisha, ix, 97
Aleppo, 5
Alibaba, ix, 21–25, 45, 46
Amazon, 133
Apple, 75, 118, 132, 133
Australia, ix, 6, 7, 22, 36, 88
Austria, 6
Autonomous driving, 77, 133

B
Balsillie, Jim, 74, 76
Bank of Montreal (BMO), 48
Bank of Nova Scotia (Scotiabank), 48
Bargaining
 negotiate, 134
 power, 133, 134
 situation(s), 134, 135
BellSouth, 74, 75
Berlin, 5
Big Six, 139
Bimpe Nkontchou, ix, 10, 16n35
Black, Asian and minority ethnic (BAME), 17n37, 49, 77
BlackBerry, ix, 75–77, 112, 118, 132
Black community, 83, 84
Black racial identity, 83, 84
Boat people, 6
Brain, 6, 23, 69, 74
Bremen, 157
Business angel(s), 26, 27, 51, 93, 96, 99, 131, 134, 141
Business Development Bank of Canada (BDC), 141
Business support programs, 142

[1] Note: Page numbers followed by 'n' refer to notes.

C
Canada, 5–7, 10, 11, 15n23, 36, 47–49, 73, 76, 77, 85, 109, 139, 140, 154–156
Canadian Imperial Bank of Commerce (CIBC), 48
Canon, 133
Capitol Hill, 87
Center for Legal Assistance to Pollution Victims, viii
Chennai, 2, 88
Chicago, 88
China, vii, ix, 21–24, 45, 46, 85, 149, 157
China pages, 21, 22, 70
Clarence Wooten, ix, 7, 88
Cloud computing, 77, 132, 133
Code-breaking skills, ix, 55, 68, 94, 99, 108, 109, 150
Code switching, 88, 91n22
Community College of Baltimore County, 8
Computer vision, 77, 133
Conestoga College, 5
Conference Board of Canada, 80n6, 156

D
Devey, Hilary, ix, 65, 69, 70n1, 70n2, 70n7, 147, 158
Discrimination
  heuristic based, 51
  prejudice based, 43, 45, 46, 49, 50
  statistical discrimination, 49
  stereotype based, ix, 43–55, 108, 109
DriveHer, ix, 97
Drones, 77, 133

E
EachNet, 24
Ecosystem(s), 28, 87, 109, 132

Enlin, Wang
  feature story, 158
Entrepreneurial alertness
  alert to opportunities, 79, 111
  associating and connecting, 78
  evaluating and judging, 78
  scanning and searching, 79
Entrepreneurs
  ethnic minority, 38, 98
  marginalized, ix, 3, 9, 12, 25, 26, 28, 29, 35–38, 43, 49, 51, 68, 69, 77–79, 84, 85, 87, 88, 91n17, 93, 96–99, 107–109, 111–114, 117, 121, 124–127, 131–134, 139–141, 145, 146
  minority, ix, 3, 9, 11, 12, 25, 26, 28, 29, 35–38, 43, 44, 46, 51, 55, 68, 69, 77–79, 83–85, 87, 88, 93, 96, 97, 99, 107–109, 111–114, 117–121, 123–127, 131–134, 139–141, 145, 146
  necessity, 10–12, 43, 48, 85, 134, 142
  opportunity, 11
  underdog, viii, 1–12, 107, 145, 147, 149–150
Envision Designs, 8
Export Development Canada (EDC), 141, 144n15

F
Facebook, 98, 118, 133
First impression, ix, 54, 94, 97, 98, 99n5
Flores, Aquilino, ix, 9, 45
Fortune 500, 1, 2, 4, 38, 124, 132, 134
France, 6
Frankfurt, 157

G
Gates, Bill, 7
George Brown College, 97

Germany, ix, 5–7, 36, 69, 73, 79, 85, 157
Google, 75, 118, 132, 133
Government support, ix, 70, 139–142
Grant(s), 127, 141, 142
Groupsite.com, 8
Guangdong (province), 157
Guangzhou (city), 157

H
The Hague, 157
Hangzhou (city), 21, 22, 88
Hannover, 157
Harvard University, 44
Heilongjiang (province), vii
Henan (province), 157
Heuristic(s), 50, 51, 54
Higher-order mental skills
  mental adaptability, 146, 147
  mental self-awareness, 146, 147
  mental strategies, 146, 147
  metacognitive skills, 146
Hoffman, Reid, 27

I
IBM, 133
Identity
  collective dimension, 84
  collective identity orientation, 84–87, 123, 124, 126, 127
  flexible identity, 91n22
  personal identity orientation, 84, 86
  role-based, 83, 84, 127
  social identity, 83, 84
  strategic identity (orientation), ix, 68, 83–88, 126, 147
ImageCafe.com, 8
Impression management
  authenticity, 96, 125
  competence, 98
  confidence, 54, 98
  credibility, 95, 96, 98
  deceptive, 101n12
  faking, 95
  first impression(s), ix, 54, 94, 97, 98
  honest, 95, 101n12
  image, 98, 99, 125–127, 134
  image discrepancy, 125
  likeability, 44
India, 2, 85
Innovation agenda, 132, 133
Internship, 10, 113
Iran, 6
Italy, 6

J
Jamaica (West Indies), 154

K
Kaifeng (city), 157
Kingston (city), 151
Kitchener (city), 5

L
Lazaridis, Mike, ix, 73, 76, 147, 158
Lazaridis, Ophelia, 76
Learning
  interpersonal learning, 38, 113
  learning-by-doing, 35–38, 113, 114
  learning from others, 37
Lebanon, 6
Legitimacy, 97, 102n19, 117, 131, 140
Leicester (Leicestershire), 96
Lewis, Reginald F., 7
LinkedIn, 27, 77, 98, 118, 120, 121

M
Ma, Jack, ix, 21, 25, 45, 70, 88, 147, 158
Machine learning, 132, 133

Mannheim, 157
Marginalized
  entrepreneurs, ix, 3, 12, 35, 36, 38, 43, 51, 68, 69, 77, 78, 85, 87, 88, 91n17, 107–109, 111, 112, 114, 121, 124–127, 134, 139, 141, 145, 146
  group(s), viii, 2, 9–11, 25, 28, 29, 35–37, 44, 49, 55, 70, 77–79, 84, 87, 88, 109, 113, 117, 123, 124, 139, 140, 146
Mekki, Remi, 5
Metacognitive, 146
Microsoft, 133, 151
MigrantHire, ix, 5, 69, 78
MindSpring, 27
Ministry of Environmental Protection, viii
Minority
  entrepreneurs, ix, 3, 12, 25–29, 35, 36, 38, 43, 44, 46, 51, 55, 68, 69, 77, 83, 85, 87, 88, 93, 94, 97–99, 107–109, 111–114, 117–121, 123–127, 139–141, 146
  groups, 9–11, 25, 28, 29, 35, 37, 43, 44, 55, 70, 77–79, 84, 87, 88, 93, 96, 97, 99, 109, 111, 113, 117, 123, 131–134, 139, 140, 146
Mobitex, 74, 75
Morgan, Clifton Roy, 153
Motorola, 74
Mulcahy, Anne, 70

N

Necessity entrepreneur(s), 10–12, 17n37, 43, 48, 85, 134, 142
Netherlands, 85, 157
Network Solutions, 8, 27

Network(s)
  brain, 69
  social, 25
New York, 1
Nooyi, Indra, 1, 12n1, 38, 88, 147, 158
  feature story, ix

O

Obama, Barack, 87
Ontario (province), 5, 73, 155
Opportunity
  alertness, 70
  entrepreneur(s), 11
Osnabrück, 157
Outsider problem
  definition, ix, 25
  discrimination, ix, 25, 108
  know-how, ix, 25, 38, 108
  network access problems, ix, 25, 30, 38, 108
  stereotypes, ix, 25, 55, 108
  stereotype threat(s), ix, 25, 108

P

Pacific Ocean, 25
Pakistan, 6
Pall-Ex, ix, 65, 67, 68, 70n1, 96
Palo Alto, 8
Patents, 133, 134, 136n8, 136n10, 136–137n11
PepsiCo, ix, 1–4, 12n1, 12n2, 12n3, 13n12, 13n13, 14n16, 14n17
Performance
  entrepreneurship, 33n28, 100n7, 101n15, 111
  learning, 25, 26, 28, 37, 38, 108, 111, 119
  personal and professional development, 69, 70, 141

Personal brand, 98, 103n24, 126
Personal qualities
 formal education or training, ix, 68
 growth mindset, ix, 68, 70, 141
 political skills, ix, 68, 141
 social skills, 68, 95
 strategic identity, ix, 68
Power, ix, 67, 76, 80n1, 131–135, 149, 153, 158
Power to Girls Foundation, ix, 97
Prejudice, 43–46, 49, 50
Private sector, 139
Progressly, 8
Purchase (city), 1

Q

Qiqihar Chemical Group (QCG), vii, viii, 149
Qiqihar (city), vii
Quaker Oats, 1, 12n1
Quantum Valley Investments, 76

R

Refugee(s), ix, 5, 6, 9, 11, 12, 14n18, 14n19, 14n20, 15n23, 36, 44, 69, 78, 79, 98, 113, 124, 127, 134, 157
Reinemund, Steven, 1, 12n4
Research In Motion (RIM), 74–76, 79n1
Royal Bank of Canada (RBC), 48
Ryerson University, 156

S

Self-regulate, 98
Serial entrepreneur, ix, 7
Shaker, Hussein, ix, 5, 14n19, 69
Signal(ing), 27, 121, 126, 133, 141, 144n13, 152

Silicon Valley, viii, 8, 15n27, 23, 28, 32n23, 44, 51, 135n7
Social capital, 29, 33n27, 33n28, 101n15, 101n16, 102n17, 103n25, 144n17
Socially adaptive, 95
Socially perceptive, 95
Software security, 77, 133, 134
Sony, 133
Stamp of approval, 141
State of the Union Address, 87
STEAM Role, ix, 8
Stereotype(s)
 heuristics, 50, 51
 stereotype threat, ix, 43–55, 85–87, 108, 109
 unconscious bias, 50
Stock market analysts, 127
Sweden, 6, 15n23
Symbol of quality, 141
System 1, 51, 98
System 2, 51, 98

T

Tacit knowledge, 35, 37, 38, 38n1
Ted Rogers School of Management, 156
Tom Online, 24
Toronto, 48, 74, 154–156
Toronto–Dominion Bank (TD), 48
Turkey, 6, 73
Twitter, 98, 118, 120, 122n8

U

Underdog(s)
 entrepreneurs, viii, 1, 9, 107, 147
 outsider problem, 107, 147
 personal qualities, 7, 107
United Kingdom (UK), ix, 6, 10, 11, 33n25, 36, 49, 77, 85

United States (US), ix, 2, 3, 6, 7, 10, 11, 15n25, 15–16n28, 21, 23, 36, 40n8, 77, 87, 88, 109, 139, 144n13
University of Waterloo, 74, 76

V
Van Street, 151, 157
Venture capital, 26, 27, 31n11, 51, 76, 93, 96, 99, 131, 135–136n7, 136–137n11, 141, 143n10, 143n11, 144n13
VentureFund.io, 8
Verisign, 8, 27
Virtual reality, 77, 133

W
Waterloo, 74, 76, 135n7

W8 Advisory, ix, 10
W. F. Herman Secondary School, 73, 76
Whitman, Meg, 12n3, 24
Windsor, 73, 74

X
Xerox, 12n3, 70

Y
Yahoo, 14n18, 24, 30n1
Yushutun (village), vii, 149

Z
Zhejiang (province), 21
Zhengzhou (city), 157

Druck:
Customized Business Services GmbH
im Auftrag der KNV-Gruppe
Ferdinand-Jühlke-Str. 7
99095 Erfurt